CITY MAPS AND STORIES
CONTEMPORARY WANDERS THROUGH THE 19TH CENTURY

ILLUSTRATED BY LORENZO PETRANTONI

TEXT BY GIANNI MORELLI

MOLESKINE

Published by Moleskine srl

Publishing Director
Roberto Di Puma

Graphic Design and Illustrations by
Lorenzo Petrantoni

Texts by
Gianni Morelli

Assistant to the Artist
William Morlacchi

Translation and Editing
ICEIGEO, Milan (Translation: Katherine M. Clifton;
text Editing: Jonathan West, Paola Paudice and Elena Rossi)

ISBN 978 88 6732 483 5

Moleskine® is a registered trademark
First edition November 2017

Printed in Italy by Galli Thierry Stampa

SUMMARY

9·17
BARCELONA

19·27
BERLIN

29·35
BUENOS AIRES

37·41
CAPETOWN

43·47
HAVANA

48·57
HONG KONG

58·65
ISTANBUL

66·77
LONDON

79·89
MILAN

91·101
NEW YORK

103·113
PARIS

114·119
SAN FRANCISCO

121·131
SAN PETERSBURG

133·139
SHANGHAI

141·149
VIENNA

THE TWENTIETH CENTURY WAS THE PERIOD APPROXIMATELY

FROM THE UPRISINGS OF 1848 TO THE FIRST WORLD WAR.

AN EXTRAORDINARY SEASON OF CULTURE,

SOCIAL TRANSFORMATIONS, MUSIC, TECHNICAL AND SCIENTIFIC

PROGRESS, DREAMS, ART, FRENZY. WE HAVE SOUGHT IT OUT

IN FIFTEEN CITIES, SCATTERED ACROSS ALL THE CONTINENTS,

ALONG THE STREETS IN WHICH THE GREATEST NOVELS

TAKE PLACE, IN THE CAFES OF THE INTELLECTUALS

WHO FORMED TWENTIETH-CENTURY PHILOSOPHY, AMID THE GOSSIP

OF THE ARISTOCRATIC SALONS AND THE POLITICS

OF THE GREAT POWERS THAT EMBRACED THE ENTIRE WORLD,

AMONGST THE RICHES OF THE NEW MIDDLE CLASSES

AND THE ART THAT CHANGED ITS FUNDAMENTAL TRAITS.

WE WILL LOOK FOR IT THROUGH THE VISIONARY STORIES

OF LORENZO PETRANTONI. LORENZO DOES NOT SIMPLY

ILLUSTRATE THE CITIES: FIRST OF ALL, HE TAKES THEM APART

AND THEN HE PUTS THEM TOGETHER AGAIN ACCORDING

TO HIS OWN PERCEPTION FULL OF SYMBOLS, DETAILS, GLYPHS,

MEANDERS, FRIEZES, SIGNS, PATHS,

AND CHARACTERS THAT ON HIS DESK ARE PROBABLY

STILL CALLED GRAPHEMES.

IN HIS ILLUSTRATIONS, OR RATHER IN HIS CITIES,

NOTHING HAPPENS BY CHANCE: IT IS ALL SELECTED,

GUIDED, TESTED, AND ONLY THEN APPROVED.

IT IS WITH THIS HELMSMAN THAT WE SET SAIL DIRECTLY

FOR SAINT PETERSBURG, DURING THE DUEL IN WHICH PUSHKIN

WAS TRACHEROUSLY SHOT BY HIS ADVERSARY, THE POMPOUS

FRENCH BARON GEORGE D'ANTHÈS, AN OFFICER

IN THE CHEVALIER GUARD REGIMENT WHO TURNED AND FIRED

BEFORE HE HAD TAKEN THE FIFTEEN STEPS AGREED.

PUSHKIN WAS FATALLY WOUNDED; HE WAS THIRTY-SEVEN,

AND MARRIED TO A WOMAN WHO WAS TOO BEAUTIFUL.

SHE WAS CALLED NATALYA.

ON THE OTHER SIDE OF EUROPE, WE GO TO PARIS,

THE THEATRE OF THE LOVE BETWEEN GEORGE SAND AND CHOPIN:

SHE WHO SMOKES IN PUBLIC, SHE WHO LEAVES HER HUSBAND,

SHE WHO IS CALLED AMANTINE-LUCILE-AURORE DUPIN

(OR DUDEVANT, HER HUSBANDS SURNAME) BUT SIGNS HER WORK

WITH A MASCULINE PSEUDONYM BECAUSE AT THAT

TIME WOMEN COULD ONLY BE WIVES OR DAUGHTERS OR MOTHERS.

THE TWENTIETH CENTURY WAS JUST STARTING AND CARS

AND MACHINES INVADED THE STREETS, FACTORIES, ROOMS... AND STORIES.

STEAMSHIPS CARRIED AGATHA CHRISTIE

TO CAPE TOWN AND KARL MARX TO LONDON. THEY TOOK CARUSO

AND SARAH BERNHARDT TO THE NEW WORLD, FROM NEW YORK

TO BUENOS AIRES: AND GRAMOPHONES CARRIED THEM

TO ALL THE REST OF THE PLANET, FROM VIENNA TO SHANGHAI.

ALSO LORENZO TAKES US EVERYWHERE, WITH HIS HUNDREDS,

EVEN THOUSANDS, OF BLACK AND WHITE PAPER FIGURES,

EACH WITH ITS OWN EMOTIONS.

THEN THE TITANIC WOULD SINK, AND ITS SOS WOULD

GO UNHEARD, BUT THIS WOULD ONLY BE A PARENTHESIS,

BECAUSE HOT-AIR BALLOONS AND THE AIRSHIPS

WOULD CONTINUE TO FLY THROUGH THE SKIES.

GIANNI MORELLI

LORENZO PETRANTONI

WAS BORN IN GENOA IN 1970.

AFTER STUDYING GRAPHIC ARTS IN MILAN,

HE MOVED TO FRANCE TO WORK AS AN ART DIRECTOR AT YOUNG&RUBICAM.

AFTER HIS RETURN TO ITALY, HE WENT ON TO WORK WITH SOME OF THE GREATEST COMMUNICATION AGENCIES.

HE THEN MOVED AWAY FROM THE ADVERTISING WORLD

IN ORDER TO FULLY DEDICATE HIS TIME TO HIS ILLUSTRATING CAREER.

HIS PASSION FOR GRAPHIC DESIGN AND HIS FASCINATION

FOR THE 18TH CENTURY COMBINE IN HIS ILLUSTRATIONS AND VIDEOS.

HE USES IMAGES FROM TEXTBOOKS AND DICTIONARIES

DATING BACK TO THAT PERIOD WHICH HE DISCOVERED WHILE BROWSING BOOKSELLERS,

GIVE LIFE BACK TO WORDS, IMAGES, EVENTS AND CHARACTERS

THAT WOULD OTHERWISE BE FORGOTTEN.

HE HAS WORKED AS A DESIGNER AND USED

HIS ART TO CREATE CAMPAIGNS AND VIDEOS FOR PRESTIGIOUS BRANDS

HE HAS WORKED WITH MAJOR NEWSPAPERS

AND INTERNATIONAL MAGAZINES

AND HE HAS HAD EXHIBITIONS ALL AROUND THE WORLD.

HE HAS WON MANY PRIZES INCLUDING

ILLUSTRATION AWARDS, LONDON INTERNATIONAL AWARDS,

NEW YORK FESTIVAL, AMERICAN ILLUSTRATION, CRESTA INTERNATIONAL ADVERTISING AWARDS, ETC.

NOW LIVES IN MILAN

HE IS A MEMBER OF THE 59ÈME DEMI BRIGADE DE LIGNE IN MARENGO

AND HE POSITIVELY LOVES PERRIER.

IN THE NINETEENTH CENTURY THE PORT OF BARCELONA WAS ONCE AGAIN ONE OF THE MOST IMPORTANT IN THE MEDITERRANEAN AFTER CENTURIES OF COMPLEX POLITICAL EVENTS LINKED TO THE SUPREMACY IN THE IBERIAN PENINSULA AND THE DISCOVERY OF AMERICA. IN THE NINETEENTH CENTURY THE INDUSTRIAL REVOLUTION BLESSED CATALONIA AND ITS CAPITAL. MODERNISM, ECLECTICISM, THE UNCONTROLLED GENIUS OF ITS ARTISTS TRAN–SFORMED THE CITY INTO A WORKSHOP OF EXPERIMENTATION AND ARCHITECTURAL "FOLLIES" THAT HAS PERHAPS NOT YET FOUND A DEFINITIVE CURE.

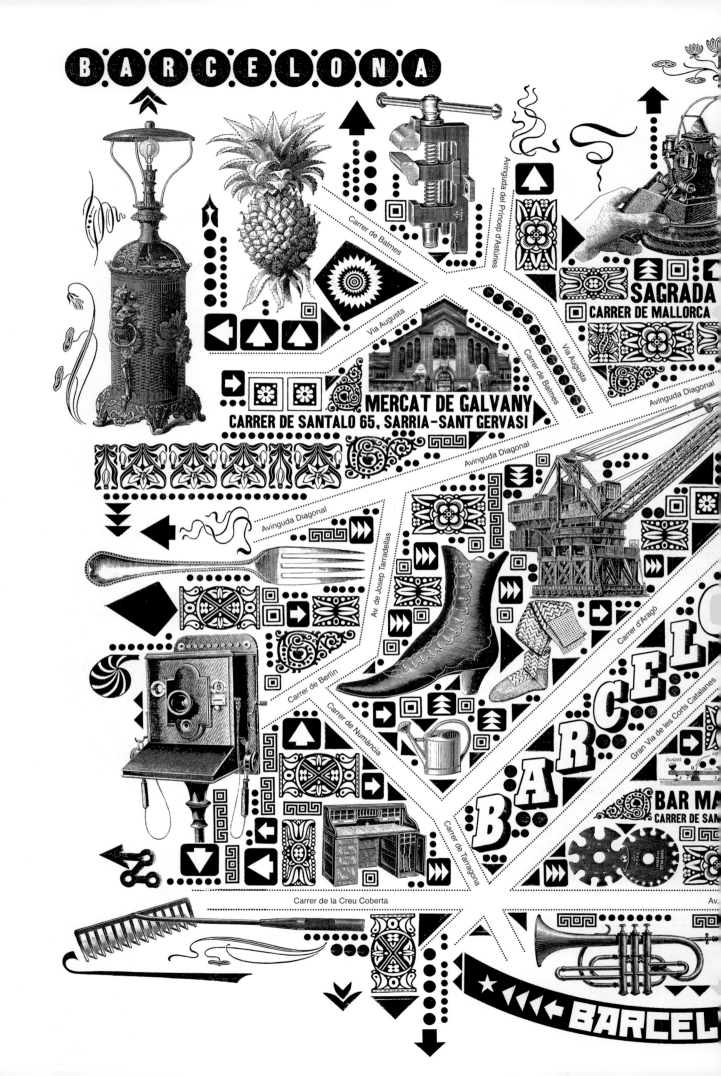

BARCELONA

MERCAT DE GALVANY
CARRER DE SANTALO 65, SARRIA–SANT GERVASI

SAGRADA
CARRER DE MALLORCA

BAR MA
CARRER DE SAN

Carrer de Balmes

Avinguda del Príncep d'Astúries

Via Augusta

Via Augusta

Carrer de Balmes

Avinguda Diagonal

Avinguda Diagonal

Avinguda Diagonal

Av. de Josep Tarradellas

Carrer de Berlín

Carrer de Numància

Carrer de Tarragona

Carrer d'Aragó

Gran Via de les Corts Catalanes

Carrer de la Creu Coberta

BARCEL

BARCEL

Passeig de Sant Joan

LIA MPLE

Avinguda Diagonal

Carrer d'Aragó

Passeig de St Joan

Gran Via de les Corts Catalanes

Carrer de Roger de Llúria

Carrer de Pau Claris

Passeig de Lluís Companys

CASTELL DELS TRES DRAGONS
PARC DE LA CIUTEDELLA, PASSEIG PICASSO 1, CIUTAT VELLA

Avinguda Meridiana

Passeig de Pujades

Carrer de la Marina

Passeig de Picasso

Via Laietana

Passeig de Circumval·lació

A

AVAL

La Rambla

Passeig d'Isabel II

CASA BRUNO CUADROS
RAMBLA, 82/PLA DE LA BOQUERIA 1, CIUTAT VELLA

BARCELONA

Passeig de Colom

Passeig de Josep Carner

BARCELONA

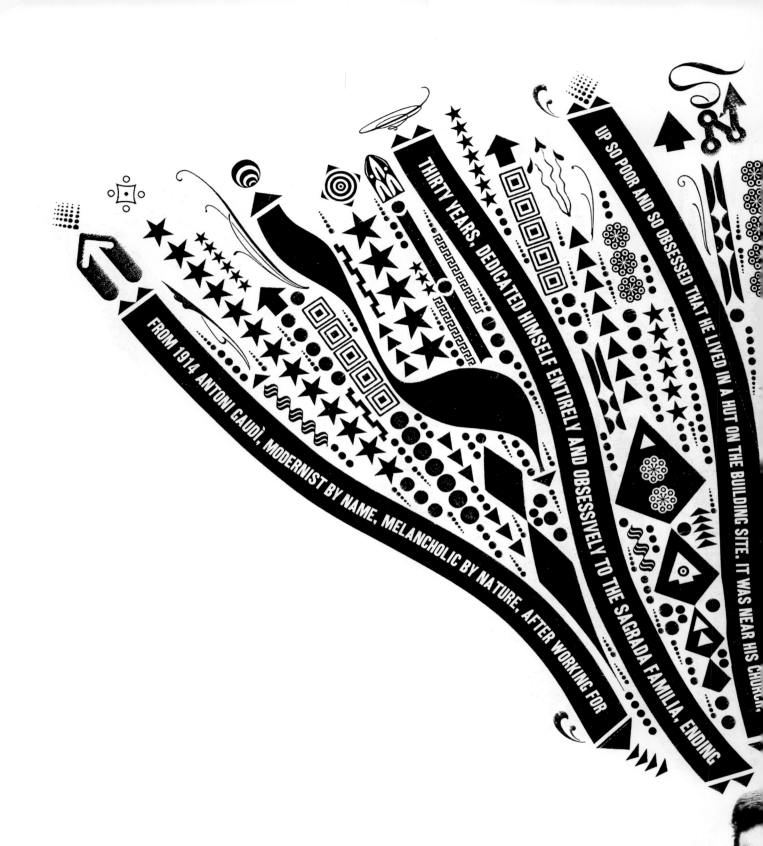

FROM 1914, ANTONI GAUDÍ, MODERNIST BY NAME, MELANCHOLIC BY NATURE, AFTER WORKING FOR

THIRTY YEARS, DEDICATED HIMSELF ENTIRELY AND OBSESSIVELY TO THE SAGRADA FAMILIA, ENDING

UP SO POOR AND SO OBSESSED THAT HE LIVED IN A HUT ON THE BUILDING SITE. IT WAS NEAR HIS CHURCH.

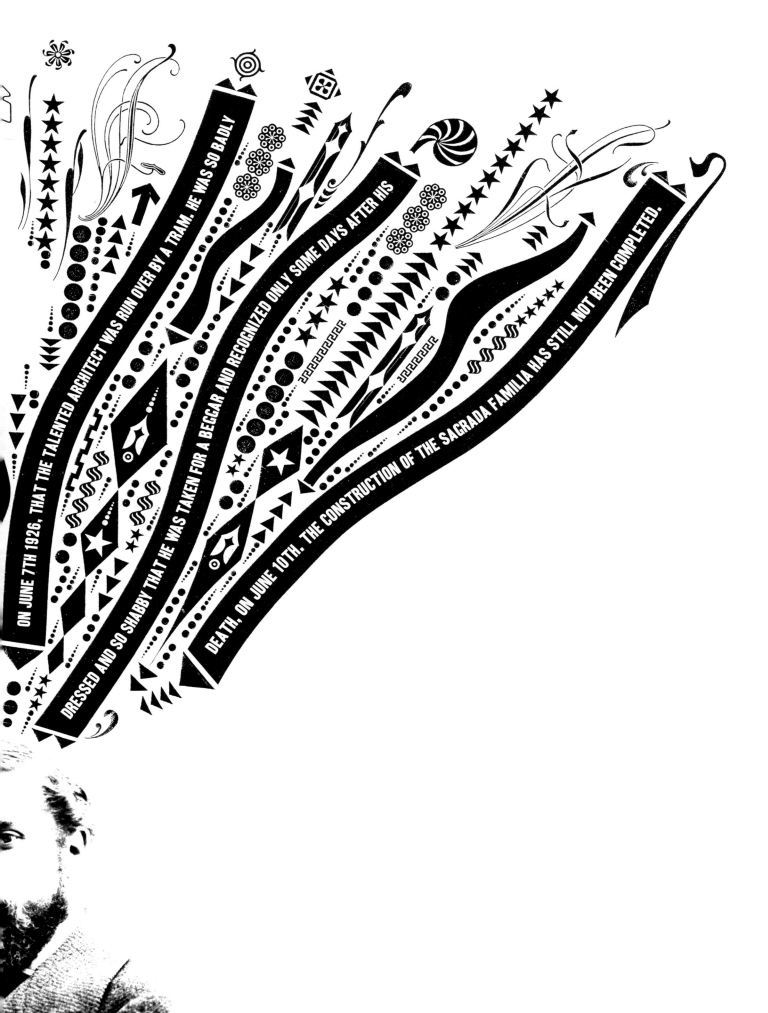

ON JUNE 7TH 1926, THAT THE TALENTED ARCHITECT WAS RUN OVER BY A TRAM. HE WAS SO BADLY

DRESSED AND SO SHABBY THAT HE WAS TAKEN FOR A BEGGAR AND RECOGNIZED ONLY SOME DAYS AFTER HIS

DEATH, ON JUNE 10TH. THE CONSTRUCTION OF THE SAGRADA FAMILIA HAS STILL NOT BEEN COMPLETED.

CASTELL DELS TRES DRAGONS

THE UNIVERSAL EXPOSITION, 1888: EIFFEL PRESENTED HIS DESIGN FOR A TOWER, BUT IT WAS

REFUSED. HE PRESENTED IT AGAIN IN PARIS, THE FOLLOWING YEAR, AND THE REST IS HISTORY.

INSTEAD OF THE TOWER, A TRIUMPHAL ARCH WAS BUILT IN BARCELONA AS THE ENTRANCE TO

PARC DE LA CIUTEDELLA, PASSEIG PICASSO 1, CIUTAT VELLA

THE EXPOSITION. THE ARCH WAS ONE OF THE FEW CONSTRUCTIONS TO SURVIVE, TOGETHER WITH THE

CASTELL DELS TRES DRAGONS, THE CASTELL THAT HOUSED THE EXHIBITION CAFÉ AND RESTAURANT.

IT LOOKS LIKE A PARODY OF A REAL CASTLE, A CREATION FOR A CARTOON, DRAWN BY A CHILD.

16

MERCAT DE GALVANY

RED BRICK, LARGE COLUMNED WINDOWS, TWO SIDE NAVES FLANKING A HIGHER CENTRAL NAVE:

FROM THE OUTSIDE IT LOOKS LIKE A CHURCH. WROUGHT IRON, GLASS, ARCHES, "PORTHOLE"

WINDOWS IN VARIOUS SHAPES: WHEN THE GATE TO THE MERCAT DE GALVANY, IN THE

SANT GERVASI–GALVANY DISTRICT, OPENS, IT IS LIKE ENTERING A SPACESHIP FROM A SCIENCE-

FICTION FILM OF A CENTURY AGO. A BLACK AND WHITE FILM TINTED WITH ARTIFICIAL HUES, AN

UNENDING SPREAD OF FRUIT, CLOTHES, MEAT, BEAUTY PRODUCTS, AND BARS WITH TABLES TO REST AT.

CARRER DE SANTALÓ 65, SARRIÀ-SANT GERVASI

BERLIN, THE CAPITAL OF THE KINGDOM OF PRUSSIA AND OF THE GERMAN EMPIRE PREPARED FOR THE FIRST WORLD WAR; IT EVOKES IMAGES OF MILITARY PARADES WITH BANDS MARCHING TO THE MUSIC OF WAGNER, IN THE SECOND HALF OF THE NINETEENTH CENTURY. ALTHOUGH THE BOMBINGS OF WORLD WAR II DESTROYED MANY OF THE BUILDINGS, STREETS, AND HISTORICAL PLACES, THE RIVER SPREE, WHICH WITNESSED ALL THIS AND MUCH MORE, CONTINUES TO FLOW QUIETLY UNDER THE BRIDGES OF GROßE BERLIN. BERLIN IS FUNDAMENTALLY A TWENTIETH-CENTURY MITTELEUROPEAN CITY.

BERLIN

BIER
KASTANIEN AL

BERLI
BERTOLT-

Perleberger Str.

Chausseestraße

Berlin-Spandau Ship Canal

Bernauer Str.

Invalidenstraße

Alt-Moabit

Reinhardtstraße

Friedrichstraße

Sprea

Unter den Li

Friedrichstraße

Straße des 17. Juni

PARISER PLATZ, MITTE
BRANDENBURGER TOR

BERLIN

Potsdamer Straße

Leipziger Str

LEIPZIGER STRAßE 16, MITTE
MUSEUM FÜR KOMMUNIKATION

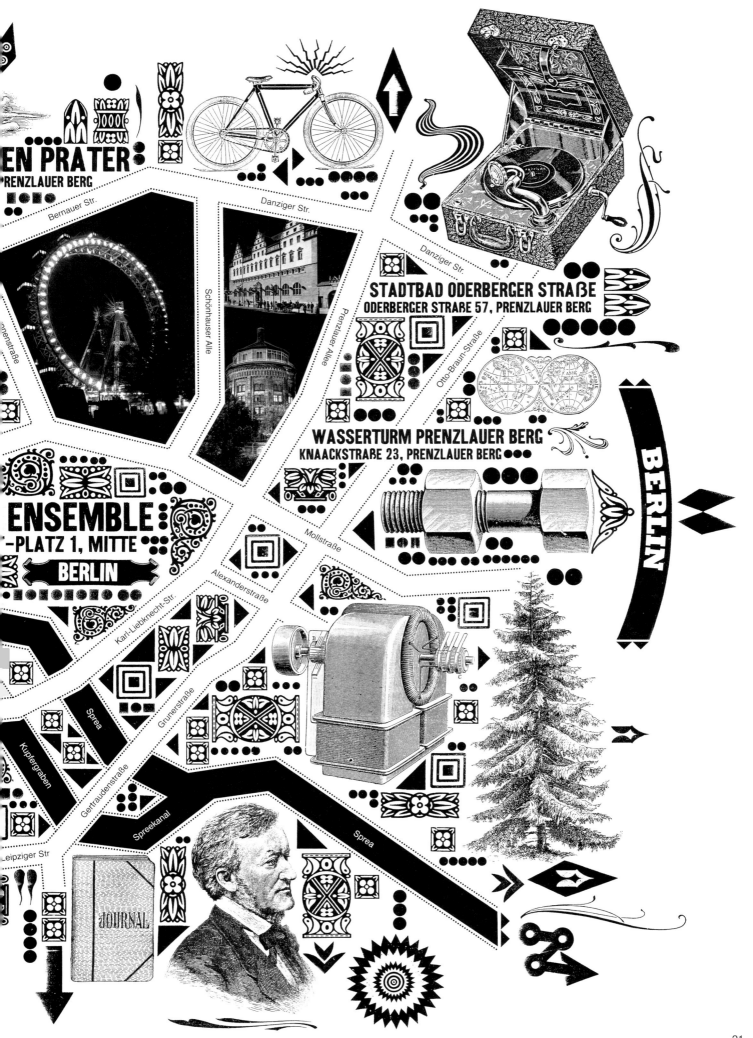

EN PRATER
RENZLAUER BERG

Bernauer Str.

Danziger Str.

Schönhauser Alle

Prenzlauer Allee

Danziger Str.

STADTBAD ODERBERGER STRASSE
ODERBERGER STRASSE 57, PRENZLAUER BERG

Otto-Braun-Straße

WASSERTURM PRENZLAUER BERG
KNAACKSTRASSE 23, PRENZLAUER BERG

ENSEMBLE
–PLATZ 1, MITTE
BERLIN

Karl-Liebknecht-Str.

Mollstraße

Alexanderstraße

Sprea

Grunerstraße

Gettraudenstraße

Kupfergraben

Spreekanal

Leipziger Str

Sprea

BERLIN

JOURNAL

THE LIEBERMANN VILLA

THE ALSEN VILLA COLONY ON THE SHORES

FOR THE UPPER CLASSES,

THROUGH A VAST PARK. ONE OF THESE WAS HOME

THE LEADER OF THE BERLIN SECESSION

SINCE IT WAS

BY THE NAZIS

...THE BERLIN SUBURB OF WANNSE

BY THE SAME NAME THAT DECIDED THE

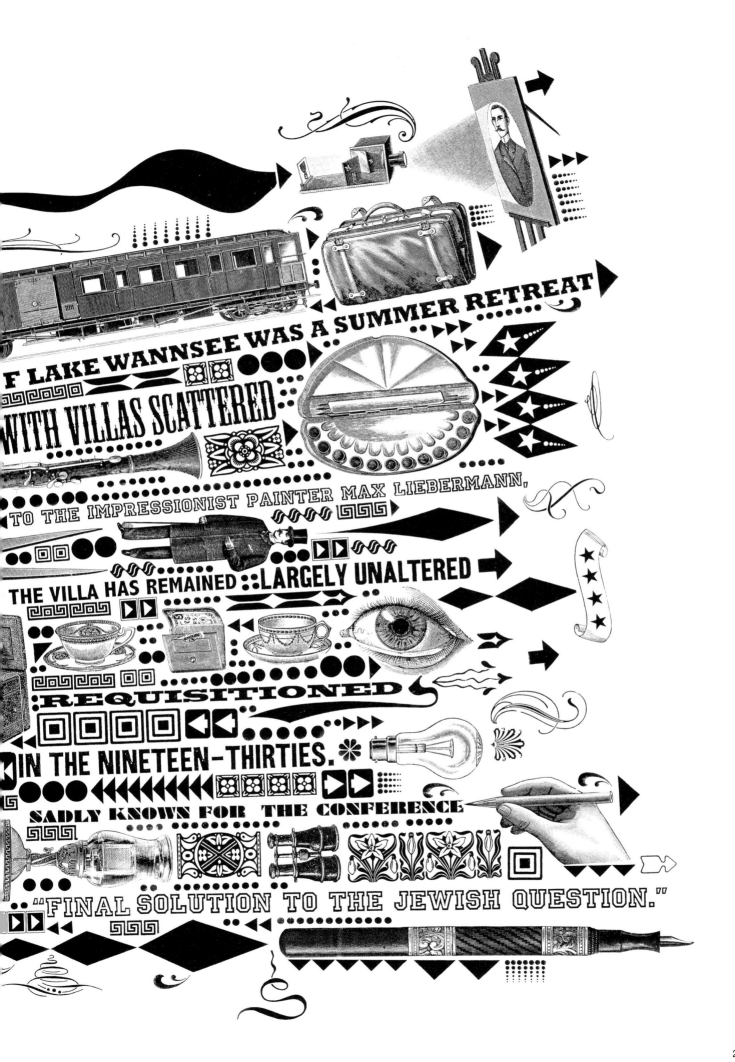

F LAKE WANNSEE WAS A SUMMER RETREAT WITH VILLAS SCATTERED TO THE IMPRESSIONIST PAINTER MAX LIEBERMANN, THE VILLA HAS REMAINED ::LARGELY UNALTERED REQUISITIONED IN THE NINETEEN-THIRTIES. SADLY KNOWN FOR THE CONFERENCE ..."FINAL SOLUTION TO THE JEWISH QUESTION."

BUND

THIS HISTORICAL BUILDING IS THE SEAT OF THE GERMAN PARLIAME
WAS OTTO VON BISMARCK, THE IRON CHANCELLOR. THE CONSTRUCTION
HALF A CENTURY TO OVERCOME THE DISAGREEMENTS BETWI
(WILHELM I AND WILHELM II). IT WAS FINALLY OPEN
OF THE GREAT WAR THE NEW CHANCELL
OF THE RECKLESS AND STRIKING WEIM

ESTAG

ONE OF THE FIRST FIGURES TO SPEAK FROM ITS WINDOWS
EDIFICE WAS PROBLEMATIC FROM THE START AND IT TOOK ALMOST
PRUSSIAN PARLIAMENT, THE CHANCELLOR AND THE EMPERORS
1894, AND IN 1918, AMONGST THE RUINS
LIPP SCHEIDEMANN PROCLAIMED THE BIRTH
PUBLIC FROM ONE OF ITS BALCONIES.

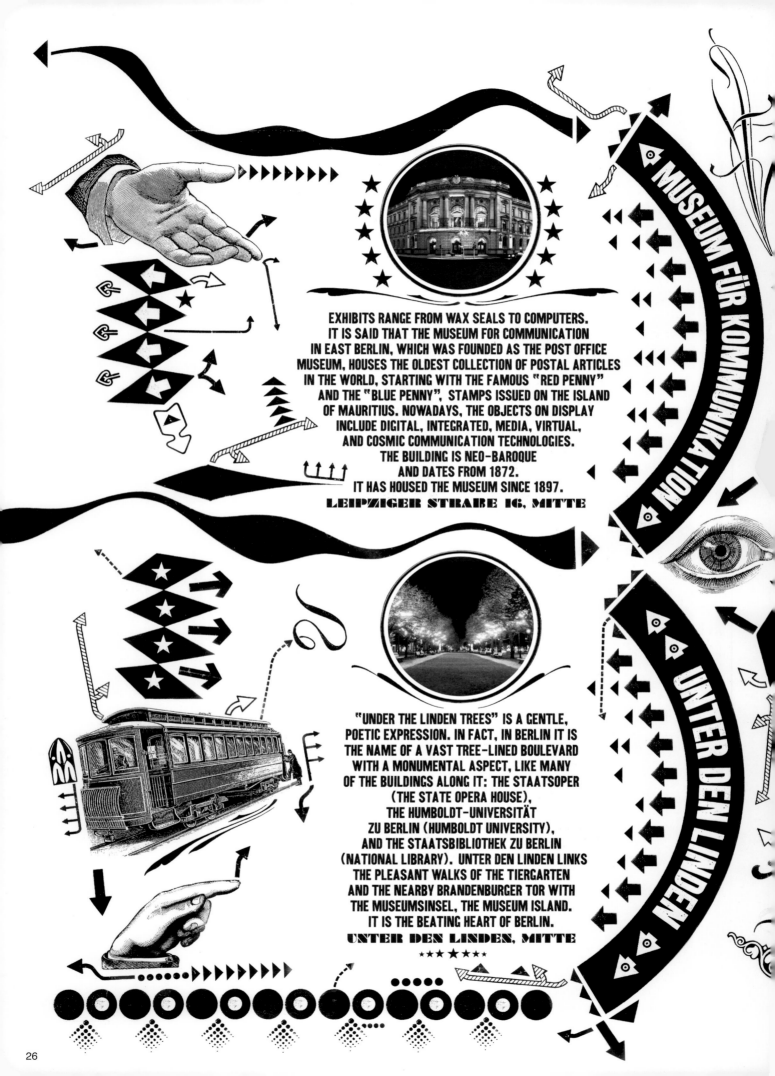

EXHIBITS RANGE FROM WAX SEALS TO COMPUTERS.
IT IS SAID THAT THE MUSEUM FOR COMMUNICATION
IN EAST BERLIN, WHICH WAS FOUNDED AS THE POST OFFICE
MUSEUM, HOUSES THE OLDEST COLLECTION OF POSTAL ARTICLES
IN THE WORLD, STARTING WITH THE FAMOUS "RED PENNY"
AND THE "BLUE PENNY", STAMPS ISSUED ON THE ISLAND
OF MAURITIUS. NOWADAYS, THE OBJECTS ON DISPLAY
INCLUDE DIGITAL, INTEGRATED, MEDIA, VIRTUAL,
AND COSMIC COMMUNICATION TECHNOLOGIES.
THE BUILDING IS NEO-BAROQUE
AND DATES FROM 1872.
IT HAS HOUSED THE MUSEUM SINCE 1897.
LEIPZIGER STRAßE 16, MITTE

MUSEUM FÜR KOMMUNIKATION

"UNDER THE LINDEN TREES" IS A GENTLE,
POETIC EXPRESSION. IN FACT, IN BERLIN IT IS
THE NAME OF A VAST TREE-LINED BOULEVARD
WITH A MONUMENTAL ASPECT, LIKE MANY
OF THE BUILDINGS ALONG IT: THE STAATSOPER
(THE STATE OPERA HOUSE),
THE HUMBOLDT-UNIVERSITÄT
ZU BERLIN (HUMBOLDT UNIVERSITY),
AND THE STAATSBIBLIOTHEK ZU BERLIN
(NATIONAL LIBRARY). UNTER DEN LINDEN LINKS
THE PLEASANT WALKS OF THE TIERGARTEN
AND THE NEARBY BRANDENBURGER TOR WITH
THE MUSEUMSINSEL, THE MUSEUM ISLAND.
IT IS THE BEATING HEART OF BERLIN.
UNTER DEN LINDEN, MITTE

UNTER DEN LINDEN

BIERGARTEN PRATER

THE OLDEST BIERGARTEN IN THE CITY (1852).
THE STREET IS KASTANIENALLEE
AND THE ESTABLISHMENT WAS FOUNDED BY HERR KALBO.
AS CAN BE SEEN FROM
THE ADDRESS, THE SLOGAN IS
"BEER UNDER THE CHESTNUT TREES".
THIS IS A BEER GARDEN, BUT
IT IS ALSO HOME TO VARIETY SHOWS,
MAY 1ST CELEBRATIONS,
A DANCE HALL, A POLITICAL HAUNT,
A THEATRE AND A CINEMA. MIRACULOUSLY,
IT SURVIVED THE BOMBINGS.

**KASTANIEN ALLEE 7/9,
PRENZLAUER BERG**

★★★★★

BRANDENBURGER TOR

ON TOP OF THE BRANDENBURG
GATE STANDS A HUGE QUADRIGA
WITH THE WINGED GODDESS OF VICTORY.
IN 1806, WHEN NAPOLEON BONAPARTE ENTERED
BERLIN AFTER OVERCOMING THE PRUSSIAN ARMY,
HE MARCHED THROUGH THE GATE IN A SYMBOLIC
ACT OF HUMILIATION OF THE OCCUPIED CITY
AND ORDERED THE QUADRIGA TO BE SENT TO PARIS.
IT WAS EIGHT YEARS BEFORE NAPOLEON WAS DEFEATED
AND THE QUADRIGA RETURNED
TO THE BRANDENBURGER TOR.
THE DORIC COLUMNS OF THIS,
THE MOST FAMOUS GATE OF BERLIN,
WERE NOT YET TWENTY YEARS OLD.

PARISER PLATZ, MITTE

★★★★★

IN THE NINETEENTH CENTURY BUENOS AIRES WELCOMED VAST NUMBERS OF MIGRANTS FROM EUROPE; BY THE END OF THE CENTURY, THE POPULATION WAS FIFTEEN TIMES MORE NUMEROUS ★ THAN AT THE START. ARGENTINA DEVELOPED, WITH TRAMS, ELECTRIC LIGHTING, THOUSANDS OF CARS, LARGE BUILDINGS, CAFÉS AND SHOPS PACKED WITH PARISIAN PERFUMES. ★ METROPOLISES IN THE WORLD. ★ THE CAPITAL OF AN IMMENSE, ALMOST UNINHABITED COUNTRY, IN THE NINETEENTH CENTURY BUENOS AIRES WELCOMED VAST NUMBERS OF MIGRANTS AT THE START OF THE NINETEENTH CENTURY, THE WAR OF LIBERATION OF THE SPANISH COLONY BEGAN IN BUENOS AIRES AND THE CAPITAL BECAME ONE OF THE LARGEST

EL ATENEO GRAND SPLENDID • AVENIDA SANTA FE 1860, RECOLETA

THIS IS WHERE THE NINETEENTH CENTURY ENDS OR THE TWENTIETH CENTURY BEGINS: IN ANY CASE, EL ATENEO GRAND SPLENDID IS ONE OF THE WONDERS TO PROPOSE TO UNESCO, TRANSFORMED INTO ONE OF THE MOST EXTRAORDINARY BOOKSHOPS IN THE WORLD. FOUR TIERS OF BALCONIES, A GREAT AUDITORIUM PACKED WITH BOOKS. THE BUILDING IS ECLECTIC IN STYLE, FROM 1919, WITH A CUPOLA FRESCO OF THE GREAT WAR; THE REST IS PURE CULTURE. THERE IS ALSO A STAGE DOTTED WITH TABLES WHERE VISITORS CAN READ OR HAVE COFFEE. ★ PARTICULARLY SINCE IT WAS ★ SPECTACULAR, VISIONARY AND THRILLING,

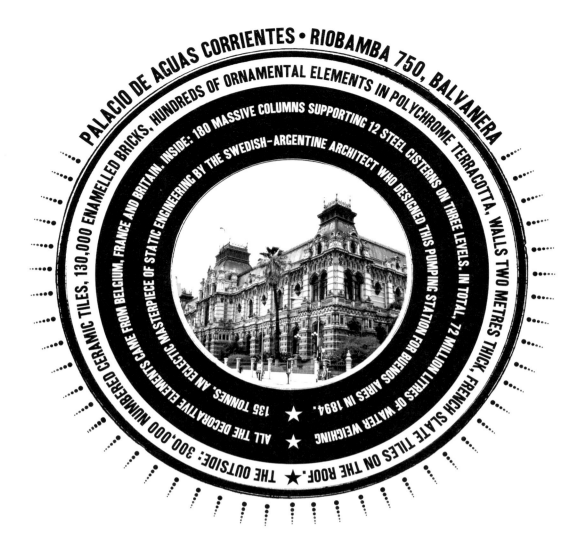

PALACIO DE AGUAS CORRIENTES • RIOBAMBA 750, BALVANERA

HUNDREDS OF ORNAMENTAL ELEMENTS IN POLYCHROME TERRACOTTA. WALLS TWO METRES THICK, FRENCH SLATE TILES ON THE ROOF. ★ THE OUTSIDE: 300,000 NUMBERED CERAMIC TILES, 130,000 ENAMELLED BRICKS, HUNDREDS OF ORNAMENTAL ELEMENTS CAME FROM BELGIUM, FRANCE AND BRITAIN. INSIDE: 180 MASSIVE COLUMNS SUPPORTING 12 STEEL CISTERNS ON THREE LEVELS. IN TOTAL, 72 MILLION LITRES OF WATER WEIGHING 135 TONNES. AN ECLECTIC MASTERPIECE OF STATIC ENGINEERING BY THE SWEDISH–ARGENTINE ARCHITECT WHO DESIGNED THIS PUMPING STATION FOR BUENOS AIRES IN 1894. ★ ALL THE DECORATIVE ELEMENTS

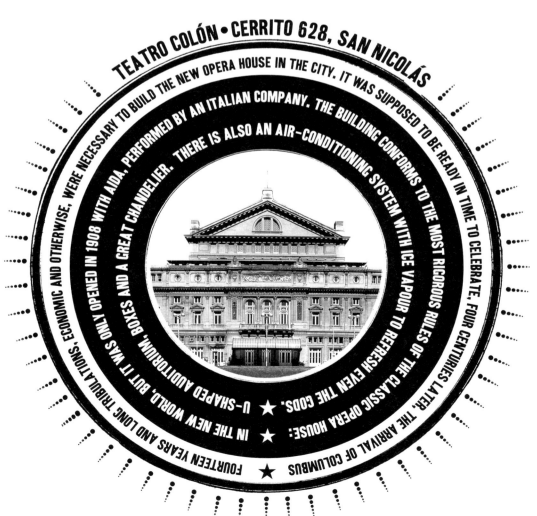

TEATRO COLÓN • CERRITO 628, SAN NICOLÁS

WERE NECESSARY TO BUILD THE NEW OPERA HOUSE IN THE CITY. IT WAS SUPPOSED TO BE READY IN TIME TO CELEBRATE, FOUR CENTURIES LATER, THE ARRIVAL OF COLUMBUS. ★ IN THE NEW WORLD, BUT IT WAS ONLY OPENED IN 1908 WITH AIDA, PERFORMED BY AN ITALIAN COMPANY. THE BUILDING CONFORMS TO THE MOST RIGOROUS RULES OF THE CLASSIC OPERA HOUSE: U-SHAPED AUDITORIUM, BOXES AND A GREAT CHANDELIER. THERE IS ALSO AN AIR-CONDITIONING SYSTEM WITH ICE VAPOUR TO REFRESH EVEN THE GODS. ★ FOURTEEN YEARS AND LONG TRIBULATIONS, ECONOMIC AND OTHERWISE,

EL ATENEO GRAND SPENDID

AVENIDA SANTA FE 1860, RECOLETA

BUENO

Av. Pueyrredón

Av. Santa Fe

Av. Callao

Uruguay

Montev

Av. Santa Fe

Av. Santa Fe

Av. Córdoba

Riobamba

Av. Callao

Av. Córdoba

Uruguay

Av. Córdoba

Av. Pueyrredón

BUENOS AIRES

Av. Corrientes

Riobamba

Av. Corrientes

Av. Callao

Av. Corrientes

PALACIO DE AGUAS CORRIENTES

RIOBAMBA 750, BALVANERA

Av. Rivadavia

Av. Rivadavia

Combate de los Pozos

Av. Entre Ríos

San José

Av. Jujuy

Av. Belgrano

A

AIRES →

Av. del Libertador

Av. 9 de Julio

Av. Santa Fe

Av. Córdoba

Av. Antártida Argentina

Av. Comodoro Py

Av. Antártida Argentina

Av. Eduardo Madero

Av. Leandro N. Alem

BUENOS AIRES

Río de la Plata

Cecilia Grierson

Av. Int. Hernan M. Giralt

TEATRO COLÓN
CERRITO 628, SAN NICOLÁS

Av. Corrientes

Av. Eduardo Madero

Av. Leandro N. Alem

Av. Alicia Moreau de Justo

BUENOS AIRES

Río Dique

CAFÉ
TORTONI

Av. Pres. Roque Sáenz Peña

1858 - 150 AÑOS

CAFE TORTONI

Av. Rivadavia

Av. 9 de Julio

IDA
AYO
825
SER

Av. Hipólito Yrigoyen

Av. Hipólito Yrigoyen

Av. Hipólito Yrigoyen

Av. Pres. Julio A. Roca

Av. Paseo Colón

Av. Ing Huergo

Azucena Villaflor

Av. Alicia Moreau de Justo

Av. Belgrano

elgrano

Av. 9 de Julio

BUENOS AIRES

PLAZA DE MAYO PEEKS FROM THE TREES AT THE END OF AVENIDA DE MAYO, LIKE THE CASA ROSADA. EVERYTHING THAT OCCURRED IN BUENOS AIRES IN 1858 WAS DISCUSSED HERE, IN FRONT OF CAFÉ TORTONI, WITH ITS DARK WOOD TABLES, WHITE-SHIRTED

ORTONI

WAITERS, AND THE MOSAIC OF
COLOURED GLASS IN THE CEILING OF
THE MAIN ROOM. AT THE TIME, NO ONE
KNEW THAT THE SIDE ROOM WOULD
BECOME A STAGE FOR TANGO UNTIL
DAWN. THE FIRST OWNER WAS CALLED
TOUAN, AND CAME FROM PARIS.

25, MONSERRAT

CAPE TOWN

THE NINETEENTH CENTURY, THE AREA OFFERED DIAMONDS AND OTHER MINERAL RICHES, NOT TO MENTION PORTS ALONG THE ROUTES TO THE EAST. IN THE BACKGROUND TOWERS THE FLAT PEAK OF TABLE MOUNTAIN AND THE SHARPER OUTLINE OF LIONS HEAD MOUNTAIN. NEARBY, THE CAPE OF GOOD HOPE DIVIDES THE OCEANS.

Kloof Nek Rd

New Church St

Whitford St

Buitengracht St

Buitensingel St

Bree St

Long St

Orange St

Orange St

Government Ave

MOUNT NELSON HOTEL

BELMOND MOUNT NELSON HOTEL – 76 ORANGE STREET, GARDENS

THE HOTEL OPENED IN 1899, JUST IN TIME TO WELCOME GENERALS, JOURNALISTS (INCLUDING THE YOUTHFUL WINSTON CHURCHILL) AND ADVENTURERS ARRIVING FROM LONDON ON THE EVE OF THE BOER WAR THAT WOULD BREAK OUT IN OCTOBER OF THE SAME YEAR. LUXURIOUS, ELEGANT, REFINED, IT IS CELEBRATED THROUGHOUT THE CITY AND IN ALL OF SOUTHERN AFRICA, AND ITS GREAT PINK BUILDING IS KNOWN AS THE PINK LADY. THE GUEST BOOK ABOUNDS WITH NAMES AND THE WALLS OF THE LIFTS ARE PAPERED WITH THE COVERS OF OLD BOOKS.

CAPE TOWN CLUB

18 QUEEN VICTORIA STREET

THE MAGNIFICENT HEADQUARTERS OF THE CAPE TOWN CLUB WAS BUILT WITHOUT SPARING EXPENSE IN 1898, ADJACENT TO THE CAPE TOWN HIGH COURT AND WAS PARTLY FINANCED BY CECIL RHODES. WITH ITS ENORMOUS WINDOWS, WHITE STONE AND VAST HALLS, THE CAPE TOWN CLUB IS THE RESULT OF A MERGER BETWEEN THE TWO MOST PRESTIGIOUS CLUBS OF THE CITY: THE CIVIL SERVICE CLUB (FOUNDED 1858) AND THE CITY CLUB (FOUNDED 1878). THE RENOWNED RESTAURANT IS ELEGANT, BUT THE WOOD PANELLED BAR IS ABSOLUTELY SPLENDID.

Strand St

Somerset Rd

Buitengracht St

Bree St

Wale St

Long St

Riebeek St

Walter Sisulu Ave

Adderley St

Heerengracht St

LONG STREET

Darling St

Strand St

A STRAIGHT STREET TWENTY BLOCKS LONG, CUTTING THROUGH THE HEART OF THE CITY AND FLANKED BY NUMEROUS VICTORIAN BUILDINGS, WITH THEIR BALCONIES, PORTICOES AND COLOURFUL WROUGHT IRON VERANDAS. LONG STREET IS MORE THAN THREE HUNDRED YEARS OLD; IT IS AS OLD AS THE CITY. ORIGINALLY, THE MERCHANTS' HOUSES, AND ALSO THE BAZAARS THAT SUPPLIED THE SHIPS TRAVELLING BETWEEN EUROPE AND THE EAST INDIES, FACED ONTO THE STREET. TODAY THERE IS A LONG SEQUENCE OF DUSTY BOOKSHOPS, ETHNIC RESTAURANTS, TRENDY BARS, JUNK SHOPS AND WINDOWS GLINTING WITH WESTERN DESIGNER PRODUCTS.

THE STATUE OF JAN VAN RIEBEECK HEERENGRACHT STREET

Hertzog Blvd

THE BRONZE STATUE OF THE FOUNDER OF CAPE TOWN, THE DUTCH COLONIST JAN VAN RIEBEECK, STANDS IN THE SQUARE OF THE ADDERLEY STREET FOUNTAIN, AT THE BEGINNING OF HEERENGRACHT STREET. IT WAS DONATED TO CAPE TOWN BY THE OMNIPRESENT CECIL RHODES IN 1899. THE FACE OF THE STATUE ALSO APPEARED ON THE OLD RAND, THE SOUTH AFRICAN CURRENCY. CURIOUSLY, THE IMAGE WAS NOT THAT OF VAN RIEBEECK, BUT RATHER THE DUTCH MERCHANT BARTHOLOMEUS VERMUYDEN, WHO NEVER SET FOOT ON AFRICAN SOIL, AND NO ONE KNOWS THE REASON FOR THE SWAP.

THIS GREAT CARIBBEAN PORT SEES HUGE SHIPS LADEN WITH GOODS SET OUT TO CROSS THE ATLANTIC. IN THE PAST, IT HAS SURVIVED EPIDEMICS,

PIRATES AND ATTACKS BY HER MAJESTYS NAVY. IN THE NINETEENTH CENTURY IT FINALLY SENT THE OFFICIALS AND THE SOLDIERS FROM MADRID

PACKING. THE LAST TRACE OF THE EMPIRE ON WHICH THE SUN NEVER SETS ON AMERICAN SOIL, AT THE START OF THE TWENTIETH CENTURY, HAVANA

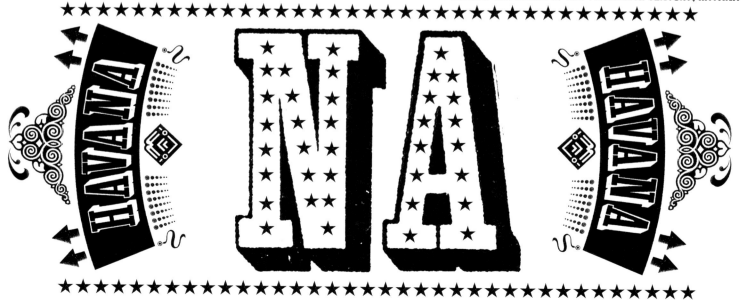

FINALLY FREED ITSELF FROM SPAIN AND FROM THE UNITED STATES, WHO HAD CRAFTILY TRIED TO REPLACE THE IBERIAN GOVERNORS.

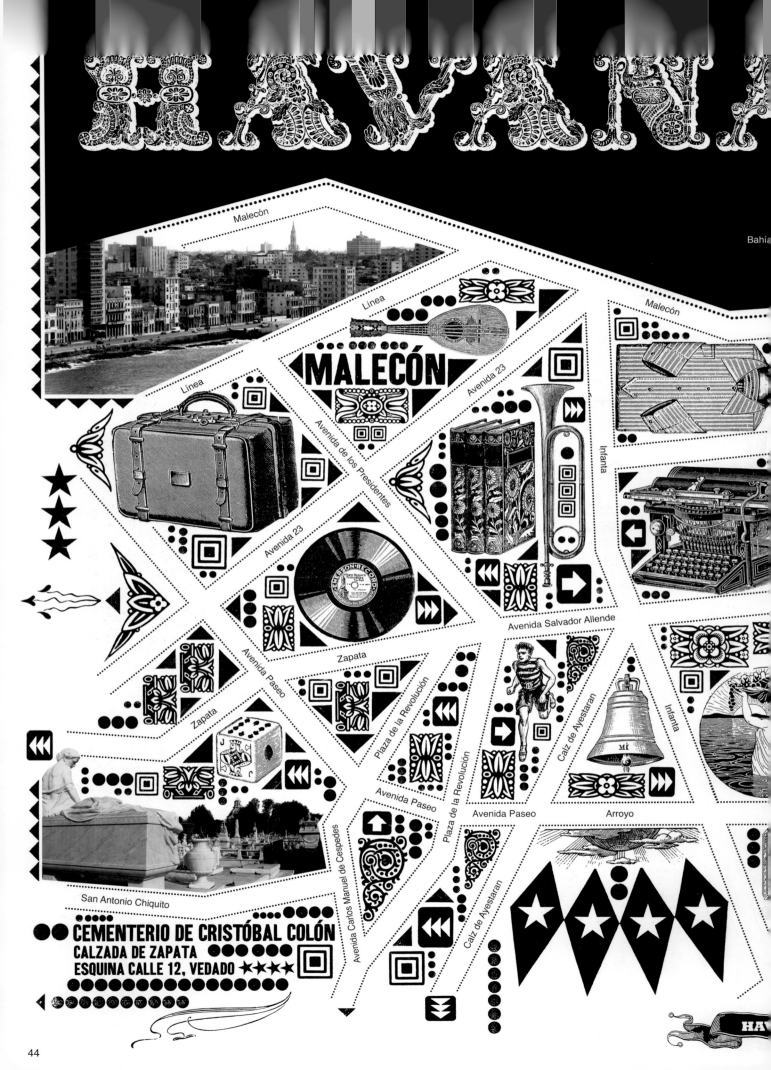

HAVANA

Malecón

Bahía

Línea

MALECÓN

Avenida 23

Malecón

Línea

Avenida de los Presidentes

Infanta

Avenida 23

Avenida Salvador Allende

Avenida Paseo

Zapata

Zapata

Plaza de la Revolución

Calz de Ayestaran

Infanta

Zapata

Avenida Paseo

Plaza de la Revolución

Avenida Paseo

Arroyo

San Antonio Chiquito

Avenida Carlos Manuel de Cespedes

Calz de Ayestaran

CEMENTERIO DE CRISTÓBAL COLÓN
CALZADA DE ZAPATA
ESQUINA CALLE 12, VEDADO ★★★★

HAV

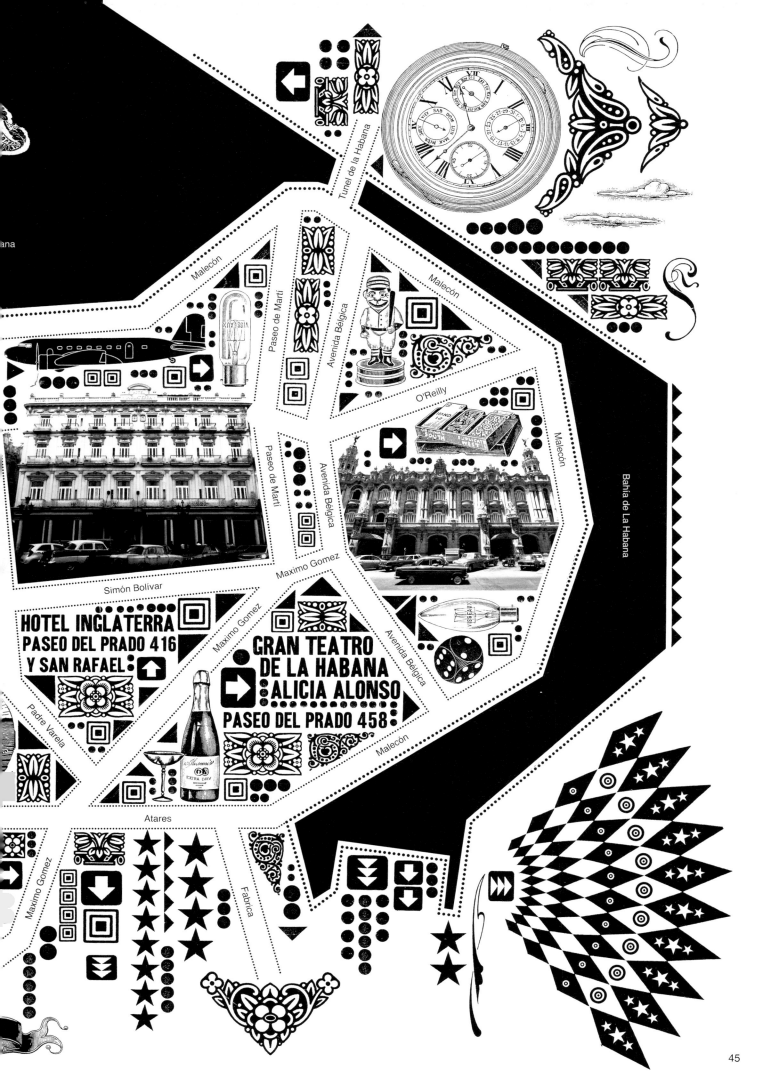

EL MALECÓN

STARTING FROM THE ENTRANCE TO THE PORT, THIS UNUSUAL, HAUNTING ESPLANADE RUNS BESIDE THE GULF OF MEXICO ALL ALONG THE NINETEENTH–CENTURY CITY (CENTRO HABANA) AND EVEN FURTHER. IN THE FIRST STRETCH EL MALECÓN (OFFICIALLY AVENIDA DE MACEO) IS PARTICULARLY PICTURESQUE; THIS SECTION WAS BUILT IN THE EARLY TWENTIETH CENTURY AND IS FLANKED BY A CONTINUOUS SERIES OF TWO–STOREY HOUSES WITH SHADY PORCHES. THE SEA BREEZES, TIME AND NEGLECT HAVE FADED THE COLOURS OF THE WALLS AND AT SUNSET IT LOOKS LIKE AN OLD THEATRE SET, WITH PAPIER MACHÉ BACKDROPS AND ABANDONED PROPS.

HOTEL INGLATERRA

ORIGINAL NINETEENTH-CENTURY MAIOLICA DECORATIONS EVERYWHERE, STUCCO AND CHANDELIERS IN THE RESTAURANT: HOTEL INGLATERRA HAS A VAGUELY MOORISH STYLE AND IS ONE OF THE OLDEST HOTELS ON THE ISLAND (1875). AMONGST ITS ILLUSTRIOUS GUESTS ARE ANTONIO MACEO, SARAH BERNHARDT AND FEDERICO GARCÍA LORCA. THE VIEW FROM THE PANORAMIC BAR ON THE TOP FLOOR IS EXCELLENT. THE PORTICO OF THE HOTEL ON PARQUE CENTRAL IS KNOWN AS THE ACERA DEL LOUVRE (THE LOUVRE PAVEMENT) AFTER THE HISTORICAL CAFÉ WHERE ARTISTS, INTELLECTUALS AND REVOLUTIONARIES USED TO MEET.

HOTEL INGLATERRA - PASEO DEL PRADO 416 Y SAN RAFAEL (BULEVAR), PARQUE CENTRAL, CENTRO HABANA

GRAN TEATRO DE LA HABANA ALICIA ALONSO

HOUSED IN A BUILDING THAT WAS ORIGINALLY A SOCIAL CENTRE FOR GALICIAN IMMIGRANTS, THE THEATRE HAS A VARIEGATED HISTORY AS A LYCEUM AND A BALLET THEATRE. THE GRAN TEATRO DE LA HABANA (LATER CALLED TEATRO GARCIA LORCA) BUILT IN 1838, WAS ENHANCED AND MODERNISED OVER THE YEARS. IT IS A HIGHLY SCENOGRAPHIC BUILDING WITH SPIRES, STATUES AND PILLARS. IT IS THE UNDOUBTED STAR OF THE PARQUE CENTRAL, THE TREE-LINED AVENUE THAT LINKS HABANA VIEJA, THE COLONIAL DISTRICT, WITH CENTRO HABANA, THE NINETEENTH-CENTURY EXPANSION OF THE CITY FOLLOWING THE DEMOLITION OF THE SPANISH WALLS.

PASEO DEL PRADO 458, PARQUE CENTRAL, CENTRO HABANA

HONG

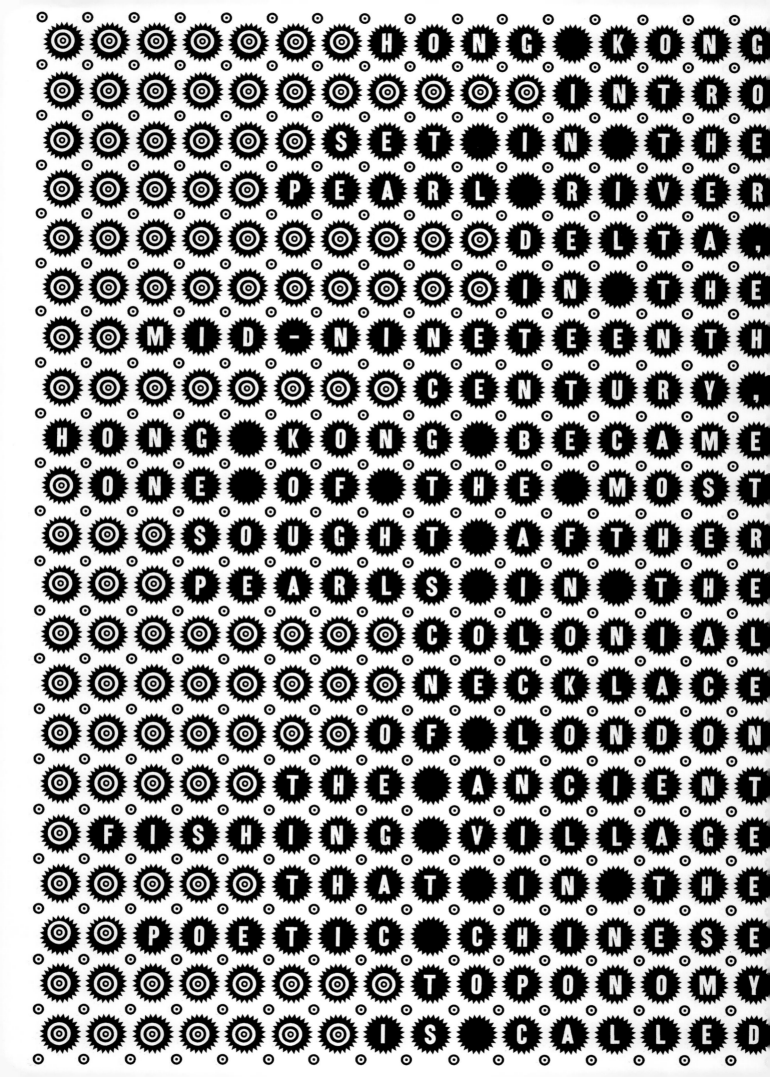

HONG KONG INTRO SET IN THE PEARL RIVER DELTA, IN THE MID-NINETEENTH CENTURY, HONG KONG BECAME ONE OF THE MOST SOUGHT AFTER PEARLS IN THE COLONIAL NECKLACE OF LONDON THE ANCIENT FISHING VILLAGE THAT IN THE POETIC CHINESE TOPONOMY IS CALLED

PERFUMED PORT, BECAME A PAWN IN THE HANDS OF THE BRITISH GUNSHIPS AND THE MERCHANTS AS THEY FOUGHT THE OPIUM WARS THAT WERE CAUSING BLOODSHED IN THE CHINA SEA IT LATER BECAME A THORN IN THE SIDE OF THE PEKING EMPIRE AND ONE OF THE GREATEST CITIES IN ASIA

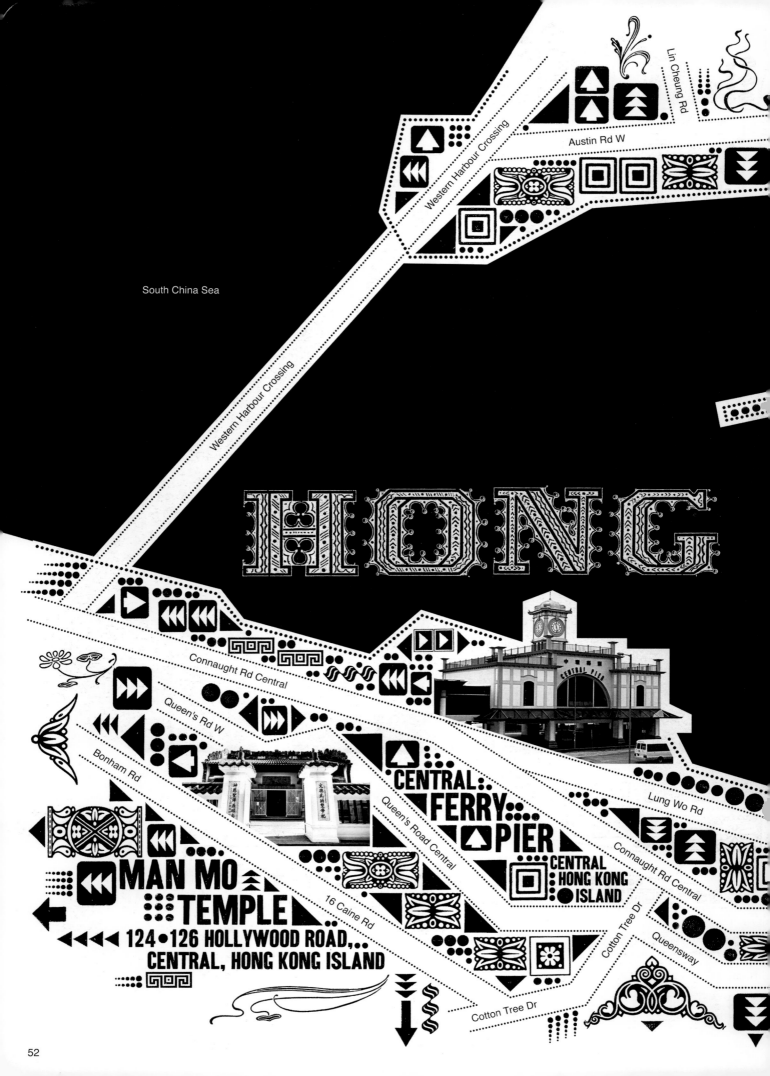

South China Sea

Western Harbour Crossing

Western Harbour Crossing

Lin Cheung Rd

Austin Rd W

HONG

Connaught Rd Central

Queen's Rd W

Bonham Rd

Queen's Road Central

16 Caine Rd

CENTRAL FERRY PIER

CENTRAL HONG KONG ISLAND

Lung Wo Rd

Connaught Rd Central

Cotton Tree Dr

Queensway

MAN MO TEMPLE

124 • 126 HOLLYWOOD ROAD, CENTRAL, HONG KONG ISLAND

Cotton Tree Dr

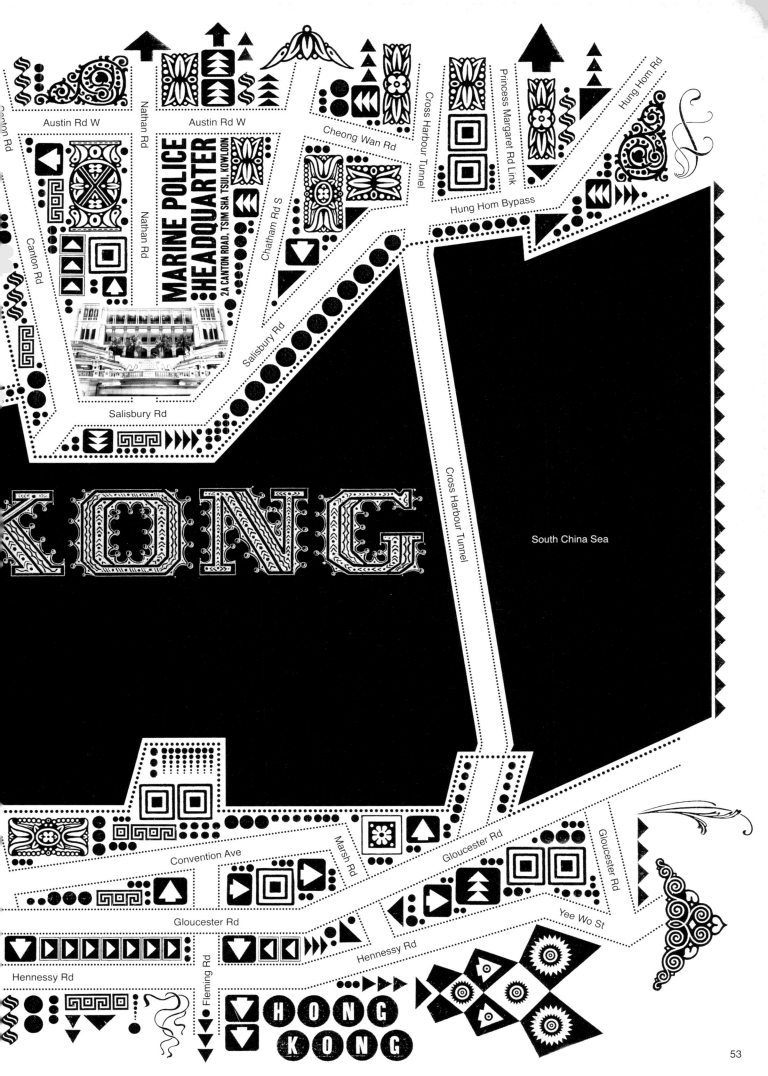

Austin Rd W

Nathan Rd

Austin Rd W

Cheong Wan Rd

Cross Harbour Tunnel

Princess Margaret Rd Link

Hung Hom Rd

Canton Rd

Nathan Rd

MARINE POLICE HEADQUARTER

2A CANTON ROAD, TSIM SHA TSUI, KOWLOON

Chatham Rd S

Hung Hom Bypass

Salisbury Rd

Salisbury Rd

Cross Harbour Tunnel

South China Sea

KONG

Convention Ave

Marsh Rd

Gloucester Rd

Gloucester Rd

Gloucester Rd

Yee Wo St

Hennessy Rd

Hennessy Rd

Fleming Rd

HONG
KONG

BETWEEN KOWLOON AND HONG KONG ISLAND. THE MORNING STAR

STEAMBOAT LEFT ONCE AN HOUR. SOME OF THE BUILDINGS REMAIN AND ARE EASILY RECOGNISABLE.

OLD S

CENTRAL,

IT IS NOT KNOWN WHETHER IT WAS ZARATHUSTRA HIMSELF WHO INSPIRED DORABJEE NAOROJEE MITHAIWALA, AN INDIAN

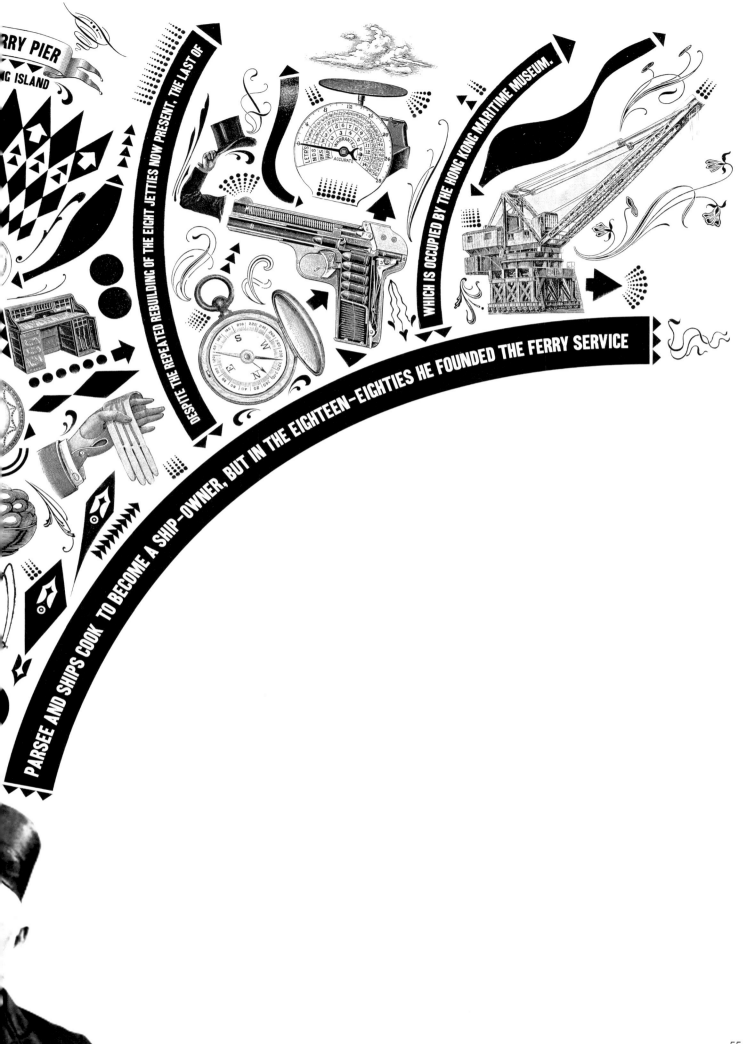

DESPITE THE REPEATED REBUILDING OF THE EIGHT JETTIES NOW PRESENT, THE LAST OF

WHICH IS OCCUPIED BY THE HONG KONG MARITIME MUSEUM.

PARSEE AND SHIPS COOK TO BECOME A SHIP-OWNER, BUT IN THE EIGHTEEN-EIGHTIES HE FOUNDED THE FERRY SERVICE

MAN, THE GOD OF LITERATURE, AND MO, THE GOD OF WAR. THIS APPARENTLY AUDACIOUS COMBINATION, PERHAPS TO SOME EXTENT OFFENSIVE, CAN BE EXPLAINED BY THE FACT THAT THE TEMPLE WAS DESTINED FOR THE PRAYERS OF STUDENTS WHO WANTED TO BECOME OFFICIALS IN THE IMPERIAL ARMY. SUCCESS IN A PARTICULARLY DIFFICULT EXAMINATION LED TO A MUCH-ENVIED POSITION. INCENSE, LACQUER, GOLD, FEW WINDOWS AND RED EVERYWHERE.

124-126 HOLLYWOOD ROAD, CENTRAL

MAN MO TEMPLE

TEN MILES FROM VICTO
HARBOUR AS THE CROW FL
IS THE SMALL ISLAN
CHEUNG CHAU, WH
CONCEALS AMONGST IT RO
THE CLAUSTROPHOBIC REF
OF THE PIRATE CHE
PO TSAI. THIS CAVE CAN O
BE REACHED BY A VERY NA
ROW PASSAGE. CHEUNG POT
WAS ONE OF THE PROTA

CHEUNG PO TS

CHEUNG PO

STS OF NINETEENTH-CENTURY
STORY AND LEGEND
THE CHINA SEA. HE WAS
E ADOPTED SON, HEIR,
VER AND RIGHT-HAND MAN
MADAME CHING, WOMAN
RATE AND WIFE OF THE
UALLY GREAT PIRATE CHENG I.
E IS SAID TO HAVE COMMAN-
O SIX HUNDRED BOATS
ID FIFTY THOUSAND MEN.

OAD, CHEUNG CHAU

TSAU CAVE

MAN CHUNG-LUEN WAS NOMINATED
MANDARIN (TAI FU) BY THE TONGZHI EMPEROR
OF THE QING DYNASTY. SHORTLY AFTERWARDS,
IN 1865, THE CHINESE YEAR OF THE WOOD OX,
THE SCHOLAR HAD THIS EXTRAORDINARY
MANSION BUILT. EVEN TODAY IT PRESERVES
MUCH OF THE ATMOSPHERE, THE COLOURS,
THE FURNISHINGS, STUCCOES, DECORATIONS,
LUXURY AND VIEWS THAT RECALL
THE CULTURED AND ARISTOCRATIC
ORIGINS OF ITS OWNER.

WING PING TSUEN, YUEN LONG DISTRICT

TAI FU TAI MANSION

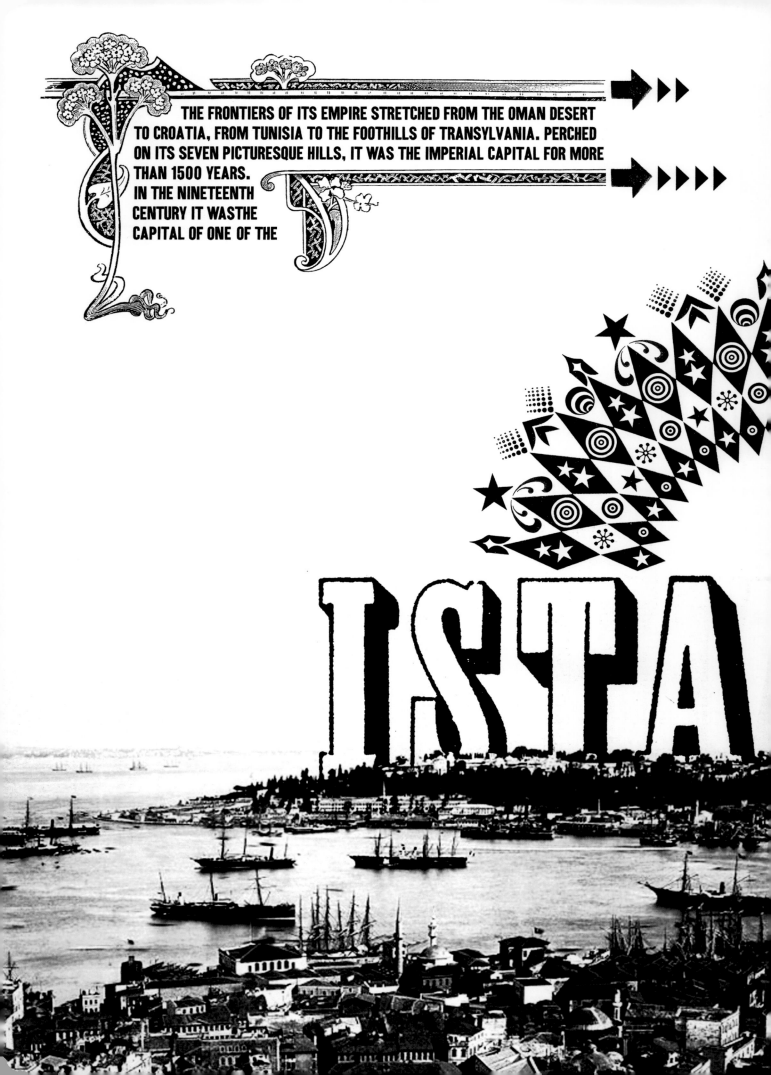

THE FRONTIERS OF ITS EMPIRE STRETCHED FROM THE OMAN DESERT TO CROATIA, FROM TUNISIA TO THE FOOTHILLS OF TRANSYLVANIA. PERCHED ON ITS SEVEN PICTURESQUE HILLS, IT WAS THE IMPERIAL CAPITAL FOR MORE THAN 1500 YEARS. IN THE NINETEENTH CENTURY IT WAS THE CAPITAL OF ONE OF THE

ISTA

MOST COSMOPOLITAN EMPIRES IN HISTORY. THANKS TO ITS GEOGRAPHICAL POSITION, IT ALWAYS PLAYED THE ROLE OF CULTURAL, MILITARY AND POLITICAL BRIDGE, EVEN AT THE START OF THE TWENTIETH CENTURY, BEFORE ONE OF THE GREATEST WARS OF ALL CHANGED EVERYTHING, ONCE AGAIN.

MESRUTIYET CADDESI 52, BEYOGLU (PERA)

PERA PALACE HOTEL JUMEIRAH

ISTIKLAL CADDESI BEYOGLU (PERA)

BEYAZIT TOWER
SÜLEYMANIYE MAHALLESI, FATIH

Alt Baruthane Cd.
Piyalepaşa Blv.
Piyalepaşa Blv.
Kurtuluş Deresi Cd.
Bülent Demir Cd.
Melek Sk.
Turabi Baba Cd.
Refik Saydam Cd.
Atatürk Köprüsü
Ragıp Gümüşpala Cd.
Galata Köprüsü
Reşadiye Cd.
Fuat Paşa Cd.
Ankara Cd.
Ebussuut Cd.
Kennedy Cd.
Kennedy Cd.
Tersane Cd.
Hamalbaşı Cd.
Boğazkesen Cd.
Kemeraltı Cd.
Tarlabaşı Blv.
Irmak Cd.
Abdülhak Hamit Cd.
Sıraselviler Cd.
Asker Ocağı Cd.
İnönü Cd.
Meclis-i Mebusan Cd.
Kadirgalar Cd.
Kadirgalar Cd.
Dolmabahçe Cd.

Marmara Denizi

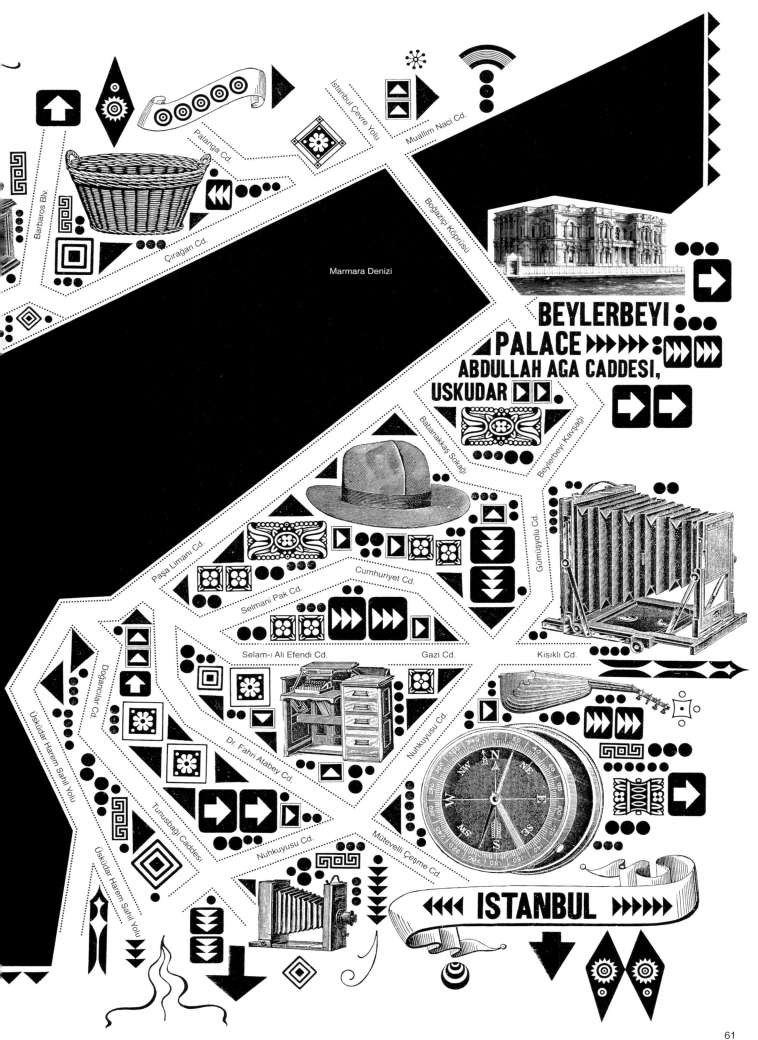

Barbaros Blv.

Palanga Cd.

İstanbul Çevre Yolu

Muallim Naci Cd.

Çırağan Cd.

Boğaziçi Köprüsü

Marmara Denizi

BEYLERBEYI PALACE ▶▶▶ ▶▶▶

ABDULLAH AGA CADDESI, USKUDAR ▷ ▷

Babanakkaş Sokağı

Beylerbeyi Kavşağı

Gümüşyolu Cd.

Paşa Limanı Cd.

Selmani Pak Cd.

Cumhuriyet Cd.

Kısıklı Cd.

Selam-ı Ali Efendi Cd.

Gazi Cd.

Doğancılar Cd.

Nuhkuyusu Cd.

Dr. Fahri Atabey Cd.

Üsküdar Harem Sahil Yolu

Tunusbağı Caddesi

Nuhkuyusu Cd.

Mütevelli Çeşme Cd.

Üsküdar Harem Sahil Yolu

◀◀◀ **ISTANBUL** ▶▶▶▶▶

BEYLERBEYI PALACE

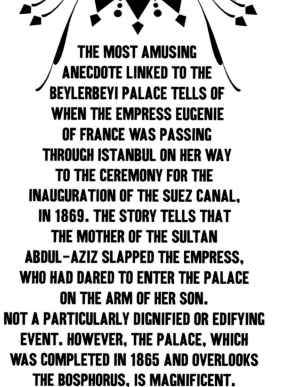

THE MOST AMUSING
ANECDOTE LINKED TO THE
BEYLERBEYI PALACE TELLS OF
WHEN THE EMPRESS EUGENIE
OF FRANCE WAS PASSING
THROUGH ISTANBUL ON HER WAY
TO THE CEREMONY FOR THE
INAUGURATION OF THE SUEZ CANAL,
IN 1869. THE STORY TELLS THAT
THE MOTHER OF THE SULTAN
ABDUL-AZIZ SLAPPED THE EMPRESS,
WHO HAD DARED TO ENTER THE PALACE
ON THE ARM OF HER SON.
NOT A PARTICULARLY DIGNIFIED OR EDIFYING
EVENT. HOWEVER, THE PALACE, WHICH
WAS COMPLETED IN 1865 AND OVERLOOKS
THE BOSPHORUS, IS MAGNIFICENT.

ABDULLAH AGA CADDESI, USKUDAR

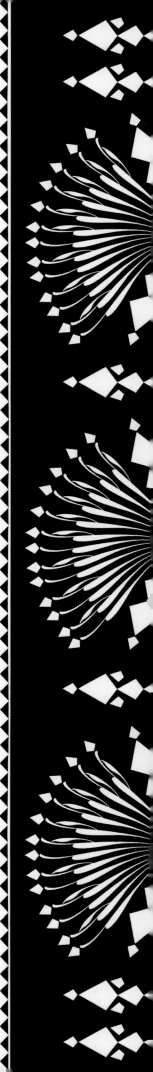

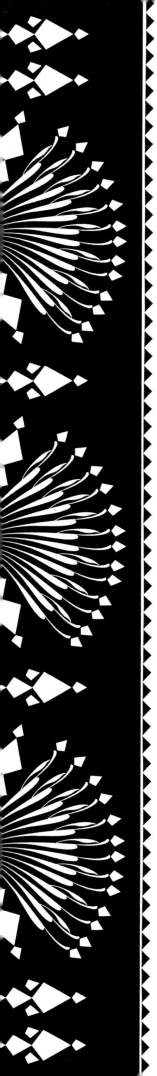

PERA PALACE

THE PERA PALACE
HOTEL OPENED IN 1892,
SHORTLY AFTER THE
COMPLETION OF THE LAST
STRETCH OF THE RAILWAY THAT
ALLOWED PASSENGERS ON THE
ORIENT EXPRESS TO REACH ISTANBUL
FROM PARIS, WITHOUT LEAVING
THE TRAIN. WITH FEW EXCEPTIONS,
THE CRÈME OF SOCIETY HAS TRAVELLED
TO ISTANBUL AND STAYED
AT THE PERA PALACE,
STARTING WITH AGATHA CHRISTIE,
WHO WAS LOOKING (OBVIOUSLY)
FOR INSPIRATION
FOR HER MURDER
ON THE ORIENT EXPRESS.

MESRUTIYET CADDESI 52, BEYOGLU (PERA)

PIERRE LOTI CAFÉ

LOTI WAS A FRENCH NAVAL OFFICER WHO HAD ALREADY TRAVELLED AS FAR AS TAHITI WHEN HE ARRIVED IN ISTANBUL. IT WAS 1876 AND PIERRE LOTI, THE FUTURE NOVELIST, FELL HEAD OVER HEELS IN LOVE WITH THE BEAUTIFUL HATIDJE. HIS DESPERATE HIDDEN PASSION INSPIRED HIS FIRST NOVEL AZIYADÉ. HE RETURNED TO ISTANBUL IN 1880, BUT SHE HAD DIED. IN THE FOLLOWING DECADES, HE OFTEN RETURNED TO A TABLE IN WHAT WOULD COME TO BE KNOWN AS PIERRE LOTI CAFÉ, WITH ITS EXTRAORDINARY PANORAMA OF THE BOSPHORUS.

PIERRE LOTI KAHVESI – EYÜP MERKEZ MAHALLESI, EYÜP

BEYAZIT TOWER

THE OLD WOODEN TOWER OF BEYAZIT, OR SERASKER
(THE WAR MINISTER UNDER THE OTTOMAN EMPIRE) BURNT DOWN,
SO IN 1828 A TOWER OF STONE AND MARBLE WAS BUILT IN THE GARDENS
OF THE MINISTRY OF WAR (NOW THE UNIVERSITY OF ISTANBUL). FROM THE HEIGHTS
OF THE HILLS OF ISTANBUL, THE TOWER (279FT TALL) WAS INTENDED TO WATCH OVER
THEBOSPHORUS, AND IN PARTICULAR FOR WILDFIRES. IN EFFECT, ON A CLEAR DAY
IT IS EVEN POSSIBLE TO SEE THE BLACK SEA FROM ITS PLATFORM.

BEYAZIT KULESI
SÜLEYMANIYE
MAHALLESI
FATIH

THE PEOPLE, THE STREETS AND THE POVERTY OF THE WORLD OF DICKENS. BUT ALSO HIS SITTING ROOMS WITH TAPESTRIED ARMCHAIRS, THE BLAZING FIRE, TEA IN BONE CHINA CUPS DECORATED WITH FLOWERS AND COLOURFUL FRUITS, OR WITH SCENES FROM THE ORIENT. THE SHADOWS, NOOKS AND CRANNIES OF JACK THE RIPPER. THE GHOSTS SO OMNIPRESENT

THAT IT IS DIFFICULT TO FIND SOMEWHERE THAT IS NOT HAUNTED. THE INDUSTRIAL WORKSHOPS LABOURING FULL TIME. THE CEREBRAL SPECULATIONS OF SHERLOCK HOLMES

OLD FATHER THAMES AND HIS BRIDGES.

THEN, ABOVE ALL, HER

QUEEN VICTORIA,

WHO EVEN GAVE

HER NAME TO

A HISTORICAL PERIOD,

TO NEW ARCHITECTURAL, ARTISTIC

AND LITERARY STYLES, AND TO A

PARTICULARLY SOBER MORALITY.

THROUGHOUT THE NINETEENTH CENTURY AND UNTIL

WORLD WAR 1, LONDON WAS THE LARGEST CITY ON

THE PLANET, IN TERMS OF BOTH POPULATION

AND POLITICAL INFLUENCE. AT THE START OF THE

TWENTIETH CENTURY, THE LONDON STOCK EXCHANGE

QUOTED A THIRD OF THE WEALTH OF THE PLANET.

LONDON

LONDON

ST PANCRAS
EUSTON ROAD

LANGHAM HOTEL
1C PORTLAND PLACE

CHARLES DICKENS MUSEUM
48 DOUGHTY STREET

NATIO
TRAF

Camden High St

York Way

Pent

Hampstead Rd

Euston Rd

Tottenham Court Rd

Theobalds Rd

Marylebone Rd

LONDON

GENERAL OMNIBUS COMPANY

Park Ln

Shaftesbury Ave

PICCADILLY CIRCUS

The Mall

Whitehall Pl

Tamigi

BUCKINGHAM PALACE
BUCKINGHAM PALACE ROAD

LONDON

LONDON

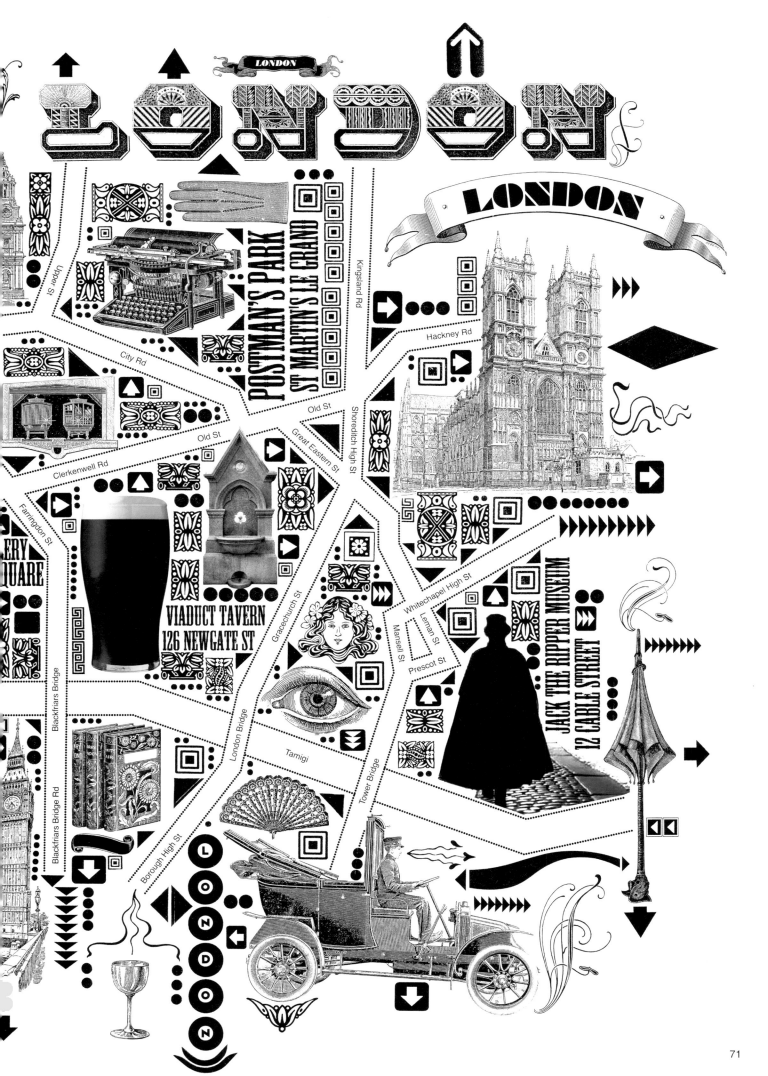

LONDON

LONDON

POSTMAN'S PARK
ST MARTIN'S LE GRAND

VIADUCT TAVERN
126 NEWGATE ST

JACK THE RIPPER MUSEUM
12 CABLE STREET

Upper St

City Rd

Clerkenwell Rd

Farringdon St

ERY
QUARE

Blackfriars Bridge

Blackfriars Bridge Rd

Old St

Old St

Great Eastern St

Gracechurch St

London Bridge

Borough High St

Tamigi

Tower Bridge

Kingsland Rd

Hackney Rd

Shoreditch High St

Whitechapel High St

Leman St

Mansell St

Prescot St

LONDON

GEORGE IV

BUCKINGHAM

SPUR ROAD

 ITS HISTORY BEGAN A COUPLE OF CENTURIES AGO, WHEN GEORGE IV
COMMISSIONED THE REFURBISHING OF BUCKINGHAM HOUSE
WHICH ONCE BELONGED TO THE DUKE OF BUCKINGHAM TO MAKE
IT A NEW ROYAL RESIDENCE. IN THE NINETEENTH CENTURY, IT HOSTED
THE LENGTHY REIGN OF QUEEN VICTORIA, WHO IS REMEMBERED
FOR HER SOBER BEHAVIOUR. CURIOUSLY, HOWEVER,
VICTORIA WAS ALSO THE OBJECT OF THE ATTENTIONS OF ONE

PALACE

COSTITUTION HILL

QUEEN VICTORIA

EDWARD JONES, WHO REPEATEDLY SNEAKED INTO THE PALACE,
STEALING VICTORIAS UNDERWEAR FROM THE ROYAL WARDROBES,
SITTING ON THE THRONE, AND HIDING UNDER THE SOFAS. IT WAS
THE EIGHTEEN FORTIES AND VICTORIA WAS A NEWLY MARRIED
TWENTY-YEAR-OLD MOTHER. EDWARD JONES NOW KNOWN
AS BOY JONES IS SAID TO HAVE BEEN EXTREMELY UGLY AND ALWAYS
DIRTY. CURIOUSLY, HE WAS ONLY FOURTEEN YEARS OLD.

HIGHGATE

IN THE UNITED KINGDOM, GHOSTS DO NOT ONLY HAUNT THE SCOTTISH CASTLES, BUT ARE ALSO TO BE FOUND IN METROPOLITAN AREAS, ON THE BORDERS WITH THE AFTERLIFE. DIAPHANOUS VAMPIRES HAVE BEEN SEEN WANDERING AT NIGHT IN THE ROADS AROUND HIGHGATE CEMETERY, AND EVEN SCOTLAND YARD HAS BEEN CALLED IN TO INVESTIGATE. THE GOTHIC TOMBS OF THE LONDON ARISTOCRACY SOMEHOW MANAGE TO RECONCILE KARL MARX WITH IMMANENCE, TRANSCENDENCE, HISTORICAL MATERIALISM AND THE BRITISH GRANDCHILDREN OF COUNT DRACULA. WHO KNOWS WHAT HE THINKS OF THE FACT THAT TO VISIT HIS TOMB, IT IS NECESSARY TO PAY 4 PER PERSON?

HIGHGATE CEMETERY, SWAINS LANE, HIGHGATE, LONDON

NATIONAL GALLERY

A COLLECTION OF WORKS OF ART, A MUSEUM, OPEN TO EVERYONE. IT WAS FOUNDED AND DEVELOPED WITH STATE FUNDING IN THE NINETEENTH CENTURY. FOR DECADES, A SUITABLE CENTRE WAS SOUGHT AND FINALLY, A PURPOSE-BUILT MUSEUM WAS DESIGNED AND CONSTRUCTED IN WHAT IS NOW TRAFALGAR SQUARE. IT HAS BEEN REPEATEDLY EXTENDED, ALTERED AND REFURBISHED TO ACCOMMODATE THE GROWING COLLECTION AND THE INCREASE IN THE NUMBER OF VISITORS. AMONGST THE MASTERPIECES HELD HERE ARE WORKS BY PAOLO UCCELLO, CÉZANNE, PIERO DELLA FRANCESCA, BOTTICELLI, MICHELANGELO, RAPHAEL, REMBRANDT, TURNER, MONET AND VAN GOGH.

NATIONAL GALLERY, TRAFALGAR SQUARE, CITY OF WESTMINSTER, LONDON

OVER 3½ FEET LONG — ONLY 99 CENTS

PRINCESS LOUISE PUB

THE MOST VICTORIAN OF THE LONDON PUBS OWES ITS NAME TO PRINCESS LOUISE, DUCHESS OF ARGYLE AND DAUGHTER OF QUEEN VICTORIA AND PRINCE ALBERT. BUILT IN 1870, IT WAS REFURBISHED IN 1891. THE EXTERIOR AND THE INTERIOR ARE NOTEWORTHY, COSY AND FRIENDLY: THE PANELLING, THE WINDOWS AND THE GENERAL DECORATION HAVE NEVER CHANGED. FOR THE GENTLEMEN, A VISIT TO THE UNUSUAL TOILETS IN COSTLY MARBLE IS A MUST. NOT FAR FROM THE BRITISH MUSEUM.

208 HIGH HOLBORN, LONDON

LONDON

CHARLES DICKENS MUSEUM

DICKENS LIVED IN THIS HOUSE FOR THIRTY-THREE YEARS, UNTIL HIS DEATH IN 1870. THESE WALLS COULD TELL ALL THE STORIES THAT RAN THROUGH THE TORMENTED AND CONTROVERSIAL LIFE OF THE MOST FAMOUS BRITISH WRITER OF THE NINETEENTH CENTURY. HERE DICKENS WROTE, AMONGST OTHERS, OLIVER TWIST AND THE PICKWICK PAPERS. IN ADDITION TO LISTENING TO THE STORIES TOLD BY THE WALLS, IT IS POSSIBLE TO EXAMINE DOCUMENTS, MANUSCRIPTS, LETTERS, PICTURES, PHOTOGRAPHS AND FAMILY POSSESSIONS.

CHARLES DICKENS MUSEUM, 48 DOUGHTY STREET, LONDON

C. BRANDAUER & Cᵒˢ Lᵗᵈ CIRCULAR POINTED PENS

PICCADILLY CIRCUS

ONE OF THE BEST-KNOWN PUBLIC SPACES IN LONDON, IT IS THE CENTRE OF A VAST AREA OF SHOPS, THEATRES AND CLUBS. THE SHAFTESBURY MEMORIAL FOUNTAIN AND STATUE STANDING IN THE CENTRE (1893) HAS A COMPLICATED AND AMUSING STORY; BRIEFLY, THE ARTIST SCULPTED ANTEROS, BUT EVERYONE TOOK IT FOR HIS BROTHER, EROS AND, DURING THE VICTORIAN ERA, IT WAS EVEN KNOWN AS THE ANGEL OF CHRISTIAN CHARITY. THE NINETEENTH-CENTURY THEATRES, THE CRITERION THEATRE AND THE LONDON PAVILION (A MUSIC HALL), OVERLOOK THE CIRCUS, BUT THE MAIN ATTRACTIONS ARE THE NEON ADVERTISING SIGNS AND THE ELEGANT SHOPS OF REGENT STREET.

PICCADILLY CIRCUS, CITY OF WESTMINSTER, LONDON

POSTMAN'S PARK

A FIFTEEN-MINUTE WALK NORTHWARDS FROM SAINT PAUL'S CATHEDRAL WILL TAKE YOU TO POSTMANS PARK; THE NAME DERIVES FROM THE FORMER GENERAL POST OFFICE THAT WAS HOUSED IN THE LARGE BUILDING NEARBY. IT HAS ALWAYS BEEN A SMALL, QUIET OASIS WITH A FEW BENCHES. THE PARK INCLUDES A LOGGIA AND A WALL ON WHICH A SERIES OF PLAQUES COMMEMORATE PEOPLE WHO SAVED THE LIVES OF OTHERS DURING SHIPWRECKS, FIRES AND OTHER DISASTERS, THE MEMORIAL TO HEROIC SELF SACRIFICE. THE ORIGINAL IDEA WAS INTRODUCED BY THE ENGLISH PAINTER GEORGE FREDERIC WATTS. BOTH THE PARK AND THE MEMORIAL DATE FROM THE END OF THE TWENTIETH CENTURY.

ST MARTINS LE GRAND, CITY OF LONDON, LONDON

SAINT PANCRAS STATION

A RED-BRICK CASTLE BUILT IN 1868, WITH A MONUMENTAL FACADE, A THOUSAND WINDOWS, A CLOCK TOWER (NOT THAT ONE) AND AN IMMENSE STEEL VAULT, SEVENTY-THREE METRES WIDE. FROM THE STREET, WE SEE WHAT WAS, UNTIL 1935, THE LUXURIOUS MIDLAND GRAND HOTEL, WHICH WELCOMED ITS GUESTS IN A LOBBY WITH RED WALLS, DOTTED WITH GOLD LEAVES AND WITH AN IMPOSING STAIRCASE THAT SEEMED TO RISE TO HEAVEN. BEHIND IT, THE VAULT, THE TRAINS, THE PLATFORMS AND TWO LOVERS, NINE METRES TALL, WHO SAY THEIR GOODBYES ON THE GRAND TERRACE.

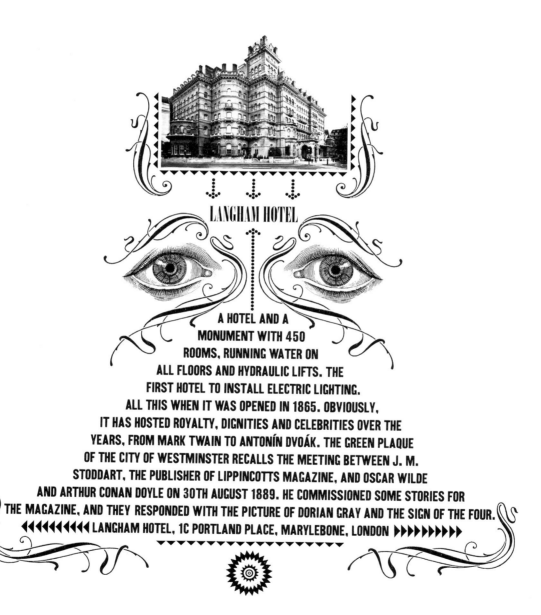

LANGHAM HOTEL

A HOTEL AND A
MONUMENT WITH 450
ROOMS, RUNNING WATER ON
ALL FLOORS AND HYDRAULIC LIFTS. THE
FIRST HOTEL TO INSTALL ELECTRIC LIGHTING.
ALL THIS WHEN IT WAS OPENED IN 1865. OBVIOUSLY,
IT HAS HOSTED ROYALTY, DIGNITIES AND CELEBRITIES OVER THE
YEARS, FROM MARK TWAIN TO ANTONÍN DVOÁK. THE GREEN PLAQUE
OF THE CITY OF WESTMINSTER RECALLS THE MEETING BETWEEN J. M.
STODDART, THE PUBLISHER OF LIPPINCOTTS MAGAZINE, AND OSCAR WILDE
AND ARTHUR CONAN DOYLE ON 30TH AUGUST 1889. HE COMMISSIONED SOME STORIES FOR
THE MAGAZINE, AND THEY RESPONDED WITH THE PICTURE OF DORIAN GRAY AND THE SIGN OF THE FOUR.
◄◄◄◄◄◄◄◄◄◄ LANGHAM HOTEL, 1C PORTLAND PLACE, MARYLEBONE, LONDON ►►►►►►►►►►

MILAN

IT WAS ALREADY THE CAPITAL OF THE PO
VALLEY, DESPITE THE FACT THAT TURIN WAS
THE CAPITAL OF THE SAVOY ROYAL FAMILY,
BUT WHEN THE DAMS BUILT ON THE RIVERS
THAT FLOW FROM THE ALPINE FOOTHILLS BEGAN
TO PUMP ELECTRIC POWER TOWARD THE PLAINS,
THE INDUSTRIAL REVOLUTION EXPLODED IN MILAN.
THE CITY HAD JUST FREED ITSELF FROM
THE HAPSBURG DYNASTY, THE GALLERIA
(ARCADES) VITTORIO EMANUELE II HAD BEEN BUILT,
AND IT HAD APPRECIATED THE NEW AND UNEXPECTED
KINGDOM OF ITALY WITH ITS CAPITAL IN PAPAL ROME.
MILAN CONTINUED TO BE INVOLVED WITH VIENNA,
PARIS AND BERLIN, BUT IT ALSO BEGAN TO LOOK SOUTH,
TOWARD THE MEDITERRANEAN.

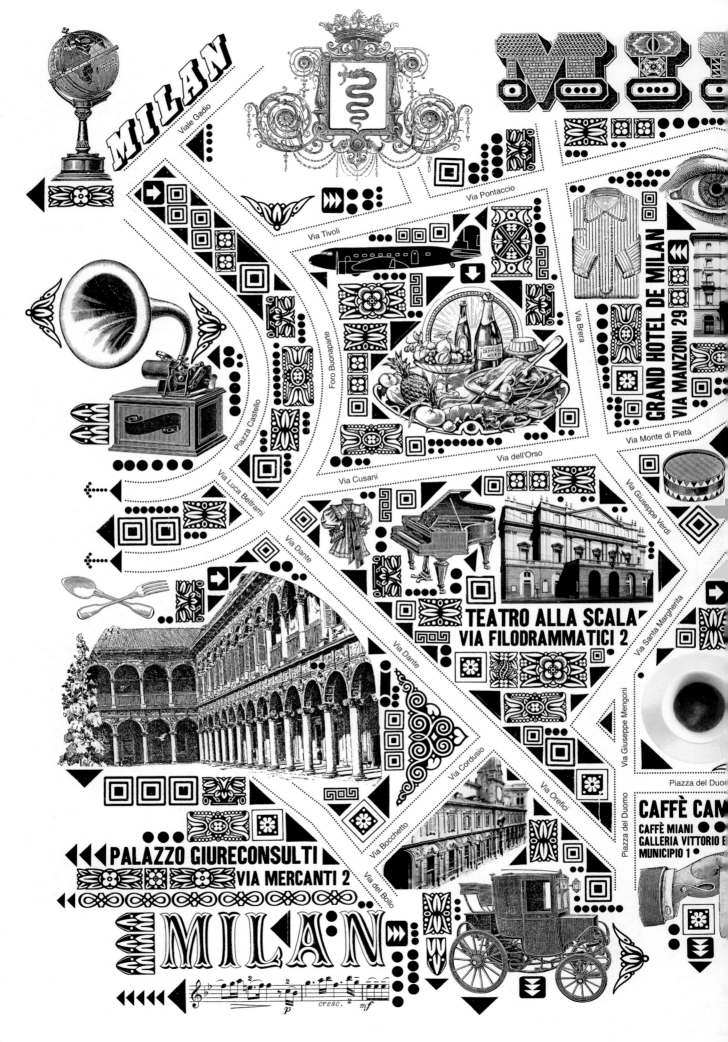

MILAN

Viale Gadio

Via Tivoli

Via Pontaccio

Via Brera

GRAND HOTEL DE MILAN
VIA MANZONI 29

Foro Buonaparte

Via Monte di Pietà

Piazza Castello

Via dell'Orso

Via Cusani

Via Luca Beltrami

Via Giuseppe Verdi

Via Dante

TEATRO ALLA SCALA
VIA FILODRAMMATICI 2

Via Santa Margherita

Via Dante

Via Giuseppe Mengoni

Via Cordusio

Via Orefici

Piazza del Duomo

Via Bocchetto

Piazza del Duomo

PALAZZO GIURECONSULTI
VIA MERCANTI 2

CAFFÈ CAM
CAFFÈ MIANI
GALLERIA VITTORIO E
MUNICIPIO 1

Via del Bollo

MILAN

cresc.

CASA MANZONI

IT IS SITUATED IN PIAZZA BELGIOIOSO, A SHORT WALK FROM THE DUOMO AND THE SCALA, AND IS A WHITE BUILDING DECORATED IN THE MID-EIGHTEENTH CENTURY IN LOMBARD NEO-RENAISSANCE STYLE. IT IS POSSIBLE TO VISIT THE ROOMS AND THE STUDY OF ALESSANDRO MANZONI, WHO LIVED HERE FOR ALMOST TWENTY-FIVE YEARS WITH HIS FAMILY. ALMOST ALL THE ITALIAN RISORGIMENTO PASSED THROUGH THESE ROOMS, FROM CARLO CATTANEO TO CAVOUR, FROM GARIBALDI TO GIUSEPPE VERDI.

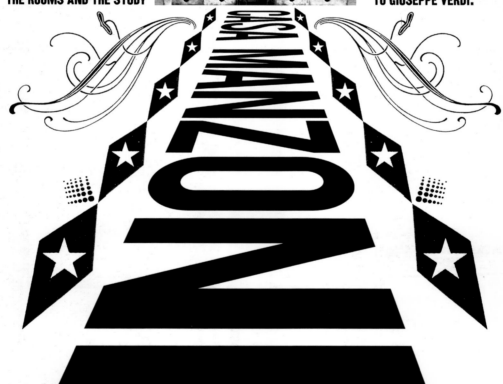

CASA MANZONI

CAFFÉ CAMPARINO

AS ONE ENTERS FROM PIAZZA DUOMO, THIS ELEGANT CAFE OCCUPIES THE LEFT-HAND CORNER OF THE GALLERIA VITTORIO EMANUELE LEADING
TO THE SCALA: THE TABLES ARE SET OUT UNDER THE PORTICO AND A SIGN WHICH SAID LIQUORERIA CAMPARI, THE EVER-PRESENT MILAN APERITIF.
IT STANDS SO CLOSE TO THE HEART OF THE CITY THAT IT HAS TOTALED ALMOST NINETY BROKEN WINDOWS DURING DEMONSTRATIONS
AND POLITICAL GATHERINGS IN THE SQUARE. A RUBY-COLOURED INSTITUTION. WITH OR WITHOUT ICE.

CAFFÉ MIANI • GALLERIA VITTORIO EMANUELE ANGOLO PIAZZA DUOMO

TEATRO A

TEATRO

TEMPL

THAT

ABUSED, B

★★★★★

AS IT IS CALLE

THE WORLD, I

OPENED IN 1778

GREW RAPIDLY I

TOGETHER WITH THE GREAT ITALIA

WITH ITS EXTRAORDINARY COMPOSER

FROM ROSSINI TO GIACOMO PUCCIN

TO TOSCANINI. "FOR ME IT IS THE FOREMOS

TEATRO ALLA SCALA

SCALA

S A WORD

OFTEN

OR LA SCALA,

THROUGHOUT

S OBLIGATORY.

THE OPERA HOUSE

QUALITY AND FAME

PERA OF THE NINETEENTH CENTURY,

ND ITS GREATEST INTERPRETERS,

FROM PAGANINI TO BENIAMINO GIGLI,

HEATRE IN THE WORLD," WROTE STENDHAL IN 1816.

VIA FILODRAMMATICI 2

VIA MANZONI 12

MUSEO POLDI PEZZOLI

ATMOSPHERE OF A GREAT PERIOD PALACE.

IN THE MID-NINETEENTH CENTURY,

FURNITURE, AND CLOCKS, IN THE ORIGINAL

COUNT GIAN GIACOMO POLDI PEZZOLI

COMPRISES JEWELLERY, CERAMICS,

WAS A GREAT TRAVELLER.

THE TIP OF AN ICEBERG THAT

HE ASSOCIATED WITH ARTISTS

AND MANTEGNA ARE MERELY

AND ARISTOCRATS OF GOOD TASTE

PIERO DELLA FRANCESCA, BOTTICELLI,

AND HAD A PASSION FOR BEAUTIFUL OBJECTS.

OBJECTS FROM DONATIONS AND BEQUESTS.

HIS COLLECTION BECAME THE EMBRYO OF ONE

HOME TO WORKS OF ART AND EXTRAORDINARY

OF THE MOST INTERESTING ITALIAN HOUSE-MUSEUMS.

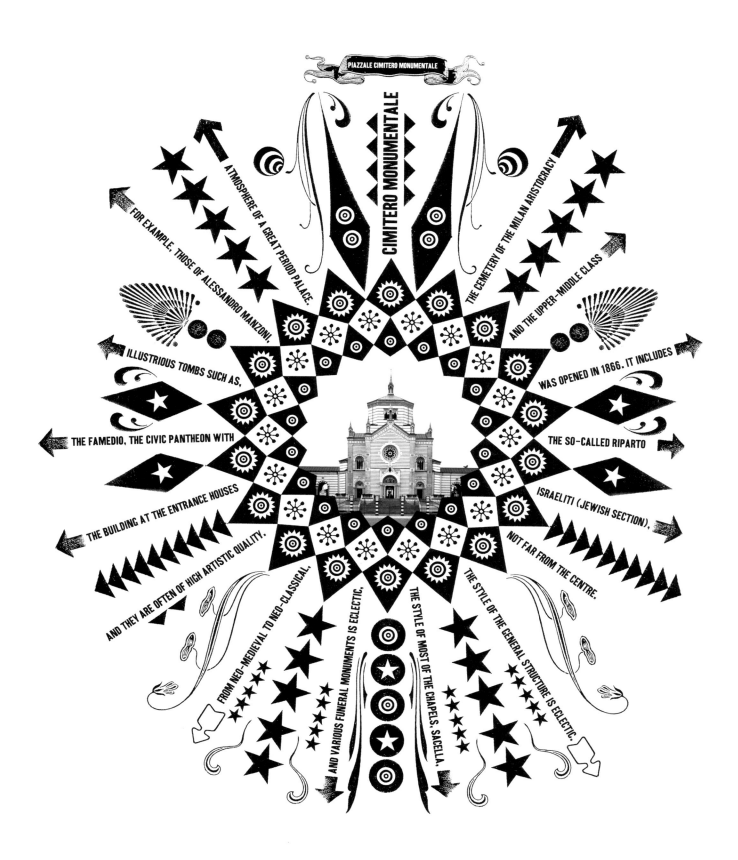

PIAZZALE CIMITERO MONUMENTALE

CIMITERO MONUMENTALE

THE CEMETERY OF THE MILAN ARISTOCRACY

AND THE UPPER-MIDDLE CLASS

WAS OPENED IN 1866. IT INCLUDES

THE SO-CALLED RIPARTO

ISRAELITI (JEWISH SECTION),

NOT FAR FROM THE CENTRE.

THE STYLE OF THE GENERAL STRUCTURE IS ECLECTIC,

THE STYLE OF MOST OF THE CHAPELS, SACELLA,

AND VARIOUS FUNERAL MONUMENTS IS ECLECTIC,

FROM NEO-MEDIEVAL TO NEO-CLASSICAL,

AND THEY ARE OFTEN OF HIGH ARTISTIC QUALITY.

THE BUILDING AT THE ENTRANCE HOUSES

THE FAMEDIO, THE CIVIC PANTHEON WITH

ILLUSTRIOUS TOMBS SUCH AS,

FOR EXAMPLE, THOSE OF ALESSANDRO MANZONI.

ATMOSPHERE OF A GREAT PERIOD PALACE.

FROM ARTISTS TO
EMPERORS: IN THE SECOND
HALF OF THE NINETEENTH CENTURY
THE ALBERGO DI MILANO NOW GRAND
HOTEL ET DE MILAN OFFERED ITS GUESTS
LUXURY, TELEGRAPH AND POSTAL SERVICES AND A
STIGLER HYDRAULIC LIFT (STILL WORKING TODAY) A
SHORT STEP FROM THE TEATRO ALLA SCALA. IT SAW
HISTORIC MOMENTS, AMONGST OTHERS WITH
THE GREAT CARUSO AND THE NEW-FANGLED
GRAMOPHONES. THE MAESTRO VERDI
DIVIDED HIS TIME FOR MORE
THAN THIRTY YEARS

GRAND HOTEL ET DE MILAN

BETWEEN HIS HOME TOWN OF BUSSETO AND SUITE 105, OVERLOOKING VIA MANZONI. FROM THE BALCONY, STANDING BESIDE THE MAESTRO, TAMAGNO SANG THE ARIAS FROM OTHELLO, WHICH HAD JUST OPENED AT LA SCALA, TO A DELIGHTED CROWD. YEARS LATER THE NEW CENTURY WAS JUST ONE YEAR OLD THE SAME STREET WAS SCATTERED WITH STRAW SO THAT THE DYING MAESTRO SHOULD NOT BE DISTURBED BY THE NOISE OF PASSING CARRIAGES. MILAN HAS ALWAYS TAKEN ITS HISTORY TO HEART.

VIA MANZONI 29, MUNICIPIO 1

NEW YORK

NEW YORK CITY

THE GATEWAY TO THE NEW WORLD, TO HOPE AND OPPORTUNITY.

THE GATEWAY TO THE COUNTRY THAT HAS THE RIGHT TO HAPPINESS RECOGNISED IN ITS CONSTITUTION.

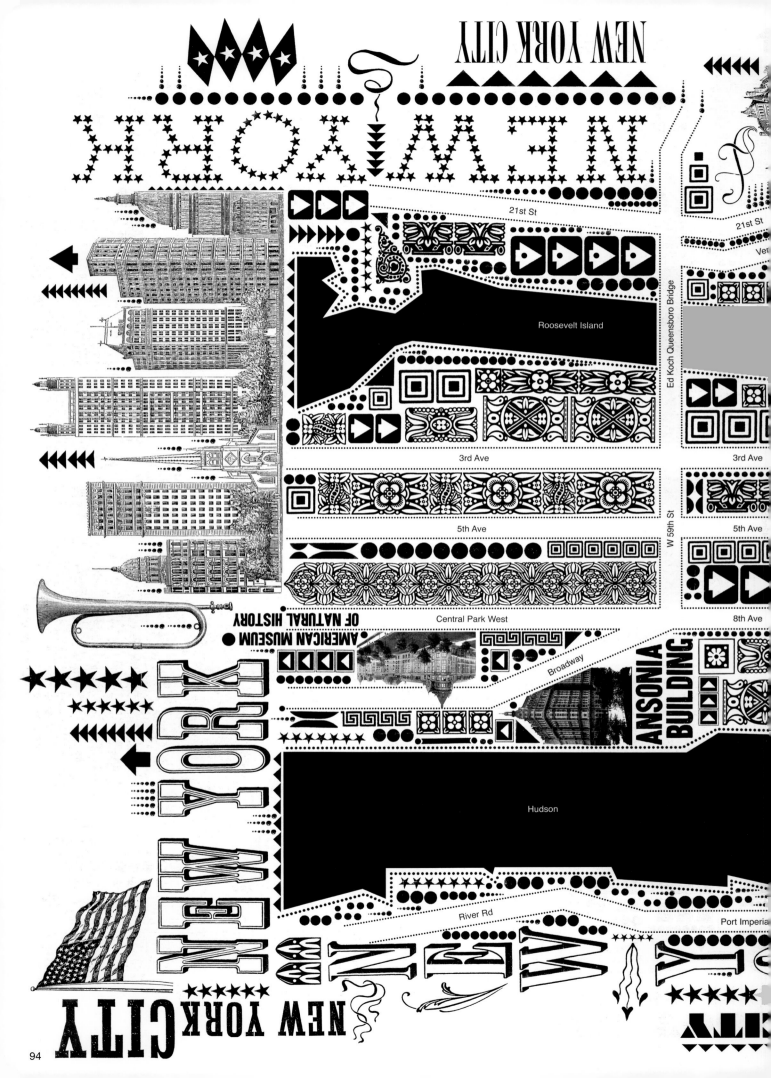

21st St

Roosevelt Island

Ed Koch Queensboro Bridge

3rd Ave

5th Ave

W 59th St

Central Park West

OF NATURAL HISTORY

AMERICAN MUSEUM

Broadway

ANSONIA BUILDING

Hudson

River Rd

Port Imperial

21st St

Ver

3rd Ave

5th Ave

8th Ave

NEW YORK

NEW YORK CITY

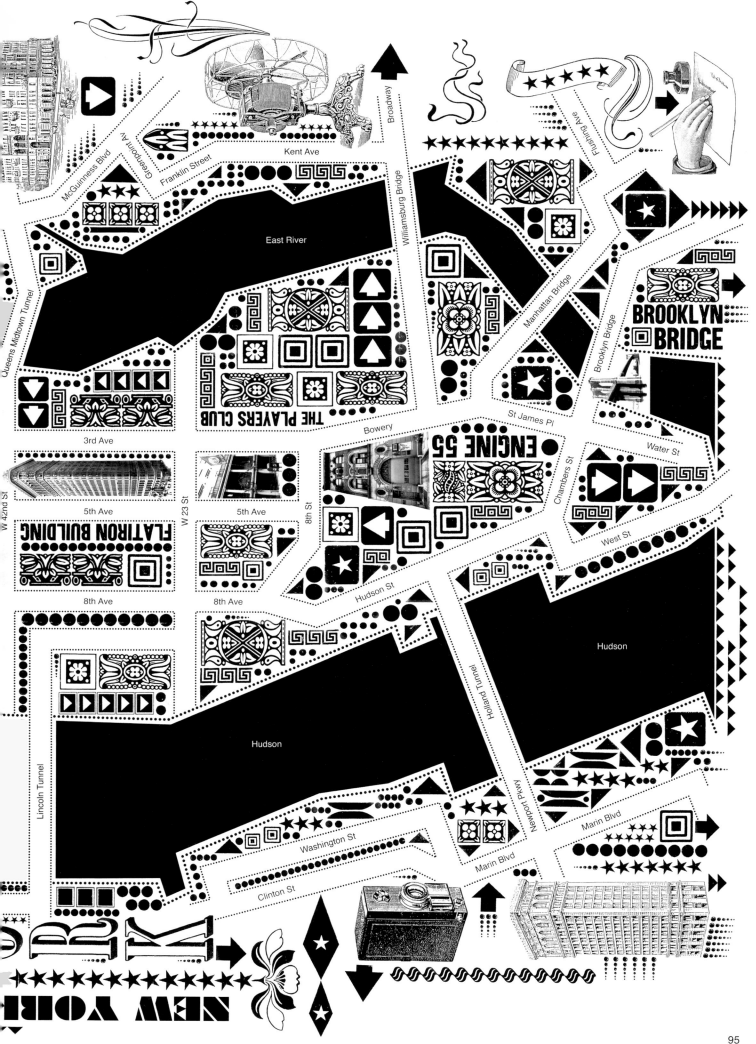

East River

Broadway

Kent Ave

Franklin Street

Greenpoint AV

McGuinness Blvd

Williamsburg Bridge

Flushing Ave

Manhattan Bridge

Brooklyn Bridge

BROOKLYN BRIDGE

Queens Midtown Tunnel

THE PLAYERS CLUB

Bowery

ENGINE 55

St James Pl

Water St

Chambers St

3rd Ave

5th Ave

W 42nd St

5th Ave

W 23 St

8th St

Hudson St

West St

FLATIRON BUILDING

8th Ave

8th Ave

Hudson

Lincoln Tunnel

Hudson

Holland Tunnel

Newport Pkwy

Marin Blvd

Washington St

Marin Blvd

Clinton St

NEW YORK

95

BROOKLYN BRIDGE

MANHATTAN, NEW YORK

DESIGNED BY THE FATHER AND COMPLETED BY THE SON FOURTEEN YEARS LATER, IN 1883, THE BROOKLYN BRIDGE WAS A REVOLUTIONARY ENGINEERING PROJECT FOR THE TIME. SIX THOUSAND FEET LONG, IT RESTS ON PNEUMATIC CAISSONS SUNK MORE THAN TWENTY METRES INTO THE RIVERBED AND IS A HYBRID CABLE-STAYED SUSPENSION BRIDGE WITH FOUR STEEL CABLES MORE THAN A KILOMETRE LONG. ONE YEAR AFTER THE INAUGURATION, IN ORDER TO OVERCOME THE PEOPLES NERVOUSNESS, JUMBO, THE SEVEN-TONNE ELEPHANT FROM BARNUMS CIRCUS, LED A PARADE OF 21 ELEPHANTS ACROSS THE BRIDGE FROM BROOKLYN TO MANHATTAN.

ANSONIA BUILDING

GRAVES AND DUBOY WERE THE ECLECTIC ARCHITECTS WHO IN 1904 SCULPTED ONE OF THE ARCHITECTURAL MASTERPIECES OF THE BIG APPLE WITH WINGS, TOWERS AND DOMES. IT WAS DUBBED THE ANSONIA BUILDING, AND THEY DESIGNED SPECTACULAR INTERIORS, TWO SWIMMING POOLS, SEALS SWIMMING IN THE FOUNTAIN IN THE HALL, MARVELLOUS STAIRCASES FANNING UP TO THE SIXTEENTH FLOOR, TOWARDS THE ROOF WHERE A SMALL FARM SUPPLIED THE TENANTS WITH FRESH EGGS. THEY ALSO INSTALLED THE FIRST AIR CONDITIONING SYSTEM IN THE CITY. THE ACOUSTIC INSULATION IS IMPECCABLE: ONE REASON CARUSO, STRAVINSKY, AND TOSCANINI RESIDED HERE.

THE ANSONIA • 2109 BROADWAY, MANHATTAN

AMERICAN MUSEUM OF NATURAL HISTORY

VISITORS TO THE AMERICAN MUSEUM OF NATURAL HISTORY ARE WELCOMED BY A FEMALE BAROSAURUS
WHO IS DEFENDING HER BABY FROM DANGER. EXACTLY WHAT THE THREAT COULD BE IS NOT CLEAR,
SINCE SHE IS ABOUT TWELVE METRES TALL, 27 METRES LONG, AND WEIGHS 25 TONNES.
SHE IS ROUGHLY 150 MILLION YEARS OLD, YET SHE IS NOT NECESSARILY THE OLDEST INHABITANT
OF THIS GREAT MUSEUM DEDICATED TO THE HISTORY OF THE EARTH.

American Museum of Natural History • Central Park West & 79th Street, Manhattan

FLATIRON BUILDING

1902: WHERE BROADWAY CUT DIAGONALLY THROUGH FIFTH AVENUE, A TWENTY-ONE STOREY RENAISSANCE REVIVAL
BUILDING WAS BUILT IN THE CURIOUS SHAPE OF A FLATIRON. IT HAD A STEEL STRUCTURE AND THE
FIRST ELECTRIC ELEVATORS. TO ANYONE ARRIVING FROM THE NORTH ON A FOGGY EVENING, THE FLATIRON
LOOKED LIKE THE PROW OF A GHOSTLY SHIP SLIPPING TOWARDS TIMES SQUARE. BREATHTAKING THE MOST
DREAMLIKE OF THE NEW YORK SKYSCRAPERS IT REALLY SEEMS TO SAIL BETWEEN THE WAVES OF THE CITY.

Flatiron Building • 175 5th Avenue, Manhattan

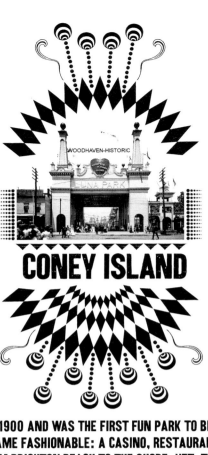

CONEY ISLAND

IT MADE ITS DEBUT IN 1900 AND WAS THE FIRST FUN PARK TO BE CALLED LUNA PARK.
CONEY ISLAND SOON BECAME FASHIONABLE: A CASINO, RESTAURANTS, BATHING RESORTS,
AND A BOULEVARD THAT LED FROM BRIGHTON BEACH TO THE SHORE. YET, THE HEYDAY DID NOT LAST LONG:
THE AREA DECLINED RAPIDLY, FILLING WITH PROSTITUTES AND PEEPSHOWS.
IT WAS NAMED THE NICKEL EMPIRE: THE PRICE OF THE TRIP PLUS A HOT DOG.

Luna Park, Coney Island • 1000 Surf Avenue, Brooklyn

THE PLAYERS CLUB

A BROWNSTONE IN GOTHIC REVIVAL STYLE DATED 1845, IT WAS REFURBISHED BY THE ARCHITECT STANFORD WHITE
FORTY YEARS LATER, BEFORE HE WAS MURDERED BY THE HUSBAND OF HIS SENSUAL MISTRESS EVELYN NESBIT,
TO ESTABLISH A SOCIAL CLUB, THE PLAYERS. THE CLUB WAS FOUNDED BY THE WELL-KNOWN ACTOR EDWIN BOOTH,
THE BROTHER OF JOHN WILKES, WHO ASSASSINATED PRESIDENT ABRAHAM LINCOLN. THE CLUB WAS MODELLED
ON THE LONDON SOCIAL CLUBS, FOR A LONG TIME WAS RESERVED FOR MEN, PREFERABLY ARTISTS, ACTORS,
WRITERS, BUT ALSO POLITICIANS AND BUSINESSMEN, PREFERABLY RICH AND FAMOUS.

The Players Club • 16, Gramercy Park (south side), Manhattan

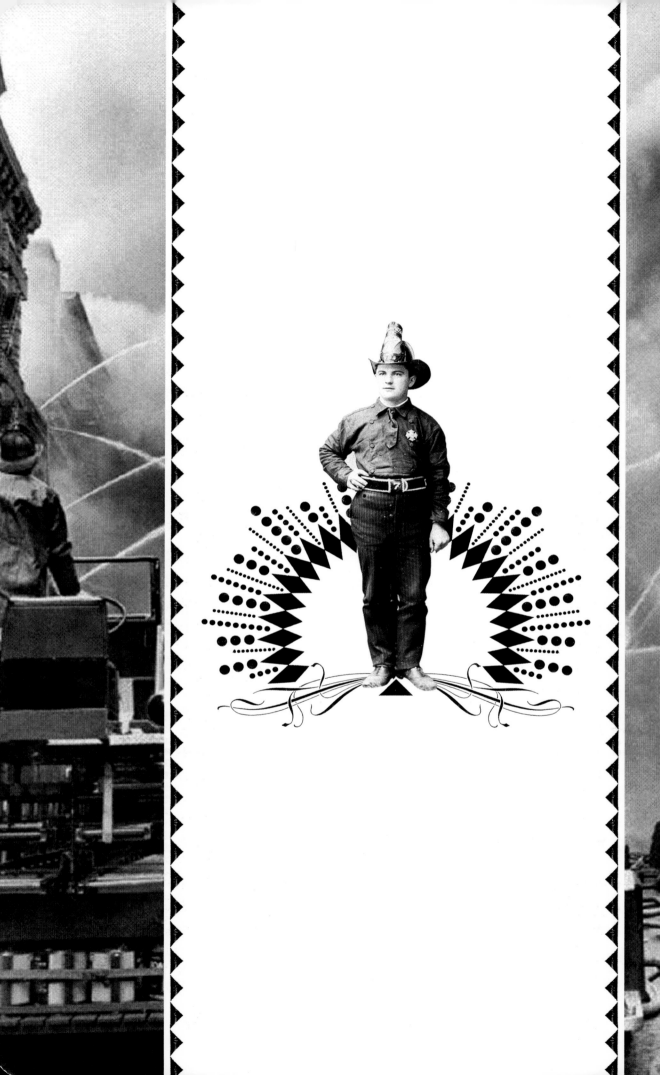
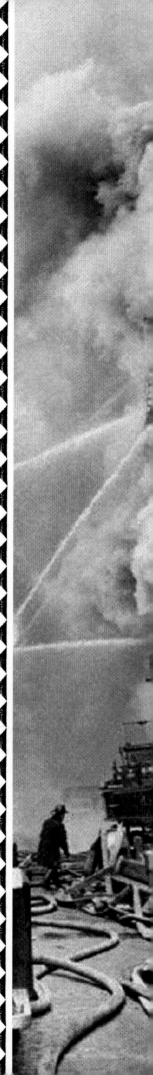

ENGINE 55

A FIREFIGHTERS STATION IN RENAISSANCE REVIVAL STYLE, PERFECTLY PRESERVED, BETWEEN LITTLE ITALY AND NOLITA. A RED AND WHITE DOOR FROM WHICH THE RED AND WHITE FIRE TRUCKS LEAVE, APPARENTLY DESIGNED PRECISELY TO MATCH IT. IN A LITTLE BUILDING THAT COULD BE THE HOUSE OF MRS SMITH. BESIDE THE DOOR WITH ITS LAMP THERE ARE VARIOUS PLAQUES TELLING THE STORY OF HEROIC DEEDS. THE NEW YORK FIREFIGHTERS HAVE ALWAYS BEEN A LEGEND.

363 BROOME STREET

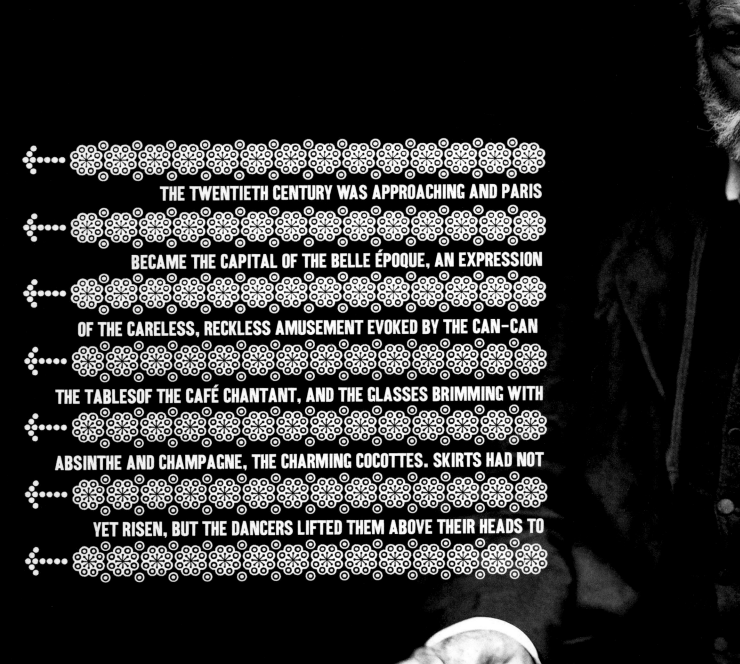

PA

THE TWENTIETH CENTURY WAS APPROACHING AND PARIS

BECAME THE CAPITAL OF THE BELLE ÉPOQUE, AN EXPRESSION

OF THE CARELESS, RECKLESS AMUSEMENT EVOKED BY THE CAN-CAN

THE TABLESOF THE CAFÉ CHANTANT, AND THE GLASSES BRIMMING WITH

ABSINTHE AND CHAMPAGNE, THE CHARMING COCOTTES. SKIRTS HAD NOT

YET RISEN, BUT THE DANCERS LIFTED THEM ABOVE THEIR HEADS TO

IS

SHOW THEIR FRILLY UNDERWEAR. ENJOYING THE SHOW WERE THE RICH

BOURGEOISIE, WHO SPENT THEIR EARNINGS FROM THE NEW

FACTORIES IN THE PRIVATE SALONS, BUT ALSO THE ARTISTS AND

INTELLECTUALS. TOWARDS THE END OF THE NINETEENTH CENTURY, PARIS

WAS NOT ONLY SYNONYMOUS WITH THE BELLE ÉPOQUE, BUT ALSO CONTINUED

TO BE ONE OF THE GREATEST ARTISTIC WORKSHOPS IN THE WORLD.

PARIS

16 RUE CHAPTAL, 75009 PARIS
MUSÉE DE LA VIE ROMANTIQUE

PARIS

Rue Lorette

Rue la Fayette

Boulevard Haussmann

Rue Pierre Charron

OPERA NATIONAL DE L

8 RUE SCRIBE, 75009

PA

Boule

PARIS

Rue des Petits Champs

Av Rapp

TOUR EIFFEL

Av de l'Opera

PARIS

TOUR EIFFEL

Pont de Carrousel

CHAMP DE MARS,
5 AVENUE ANATOLE FRANCE, 75007

LE BON MARCHÉ
24 RUE DE SÈVRES,
75007 PARIS

Rue Mazarine

CAFÉ PROCOPE TENU PAR ZOPPI

Rue de Babylone

Boulevard Saint-Germain

Rue de Condé

PROCOPE

Rue de Sèvres

Rue d'Assas

PARIS

PARIS

JARDIN DU LUXEMBOURG

Rue Gay-Lu

PETROLEA

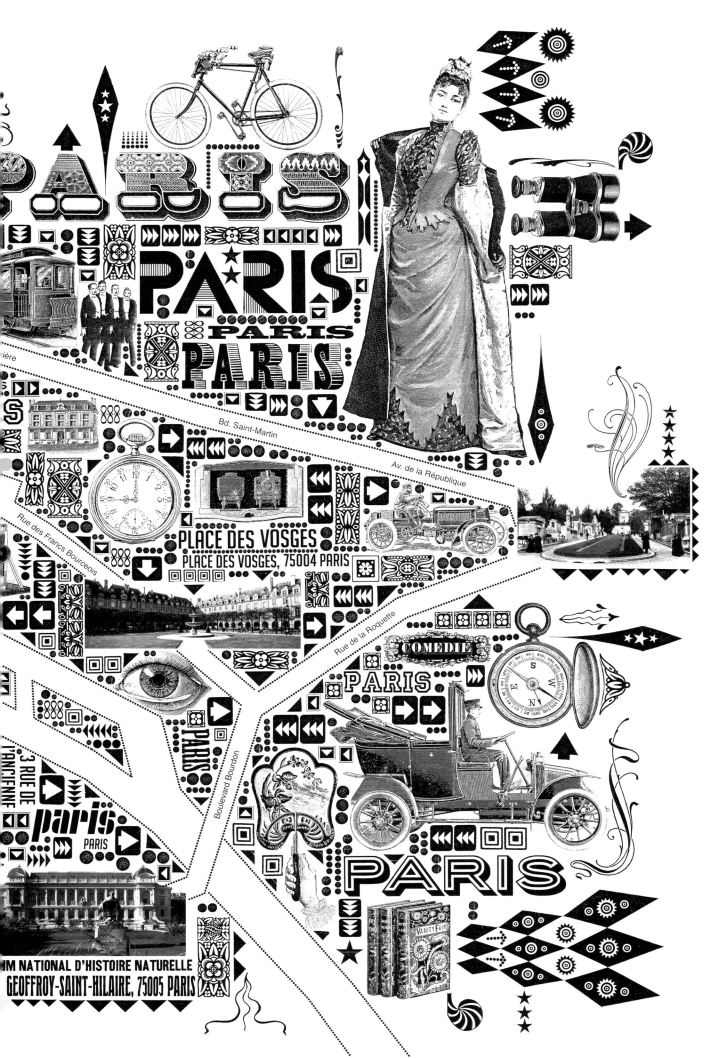

PARIS

PARIS
PARIS
PARIS

Bd. Saint-Martin

Av. de la République

PLACE DES VOSGES
PLACE DES VOSGES, 75004 PARIS

Rue des Francs Bourgeois

Rue de la Roquette

COMEDIE

PARIS

PARIS

Boulevard Bourdon

3 RUE DE L'ANCIENNE

paris
PARIS

VANITY FAIR

PARIS

UM NATIONAL D'HISTOIRE NATURELLE
GEOFFROY-SAINT-HILAIRE, 75005 PARIS

IN THE SECOND HALF OF THE NINETEENTH CENTURY, TO BE PRECISE IN 1869, THE FOLIES BERGÈRE WAS BORN. PARIS WAS DAZED WITH CHAMPAGNE AND THE CAN CAN, AND THE CLUB BECAME ONE OF THE LEGENDS OF THE BELLE EPOQUE. THE MAIN PURPOSE OF THE CAN CAN WAS TO DISPLAY THE UNDERWEAR OF THE DANCERS, TO SCANDALISE AND DELIGHT AN EVER-EXCITED AUDIENCE. IN THE LAST YEARS OF THE CENTURY, THE UNDERWEAR WAS MINIMAL AND TOPLESS DANCING WHICH

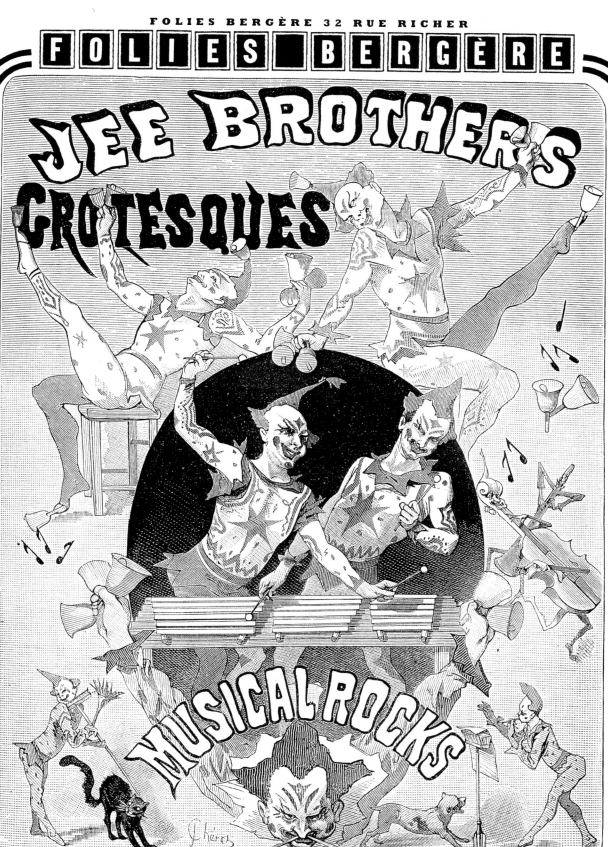

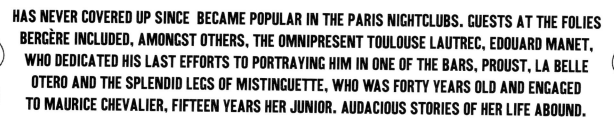

HAS NEVER COVERED UP SINCE BECAME POPULAR IN THE PARIS NIGHTCLUBS. GUESTS AT THE FOLIES BERGÈRE INCLUDED, AMONGST OTHERS, THE OMNIPRESENT TOULOUSE LAUTREC, EDOUARD MANET, WHO DEDICATED HIS LAST EFFORTS TO PORTRAYING HIM IN ONE OF THE BARS, PROUST, LA BELLE OTERO AND THE SPLENDID LEGS OF MISTINGUETTE, WHO WAS FORTY YEARS OLD AND ENGAGED TO MAURICE CHEVALIER, FIFTEEN YEARS HER JUNIOR. AUDACIOUS STORIES OF HER LIFE ABOUND.

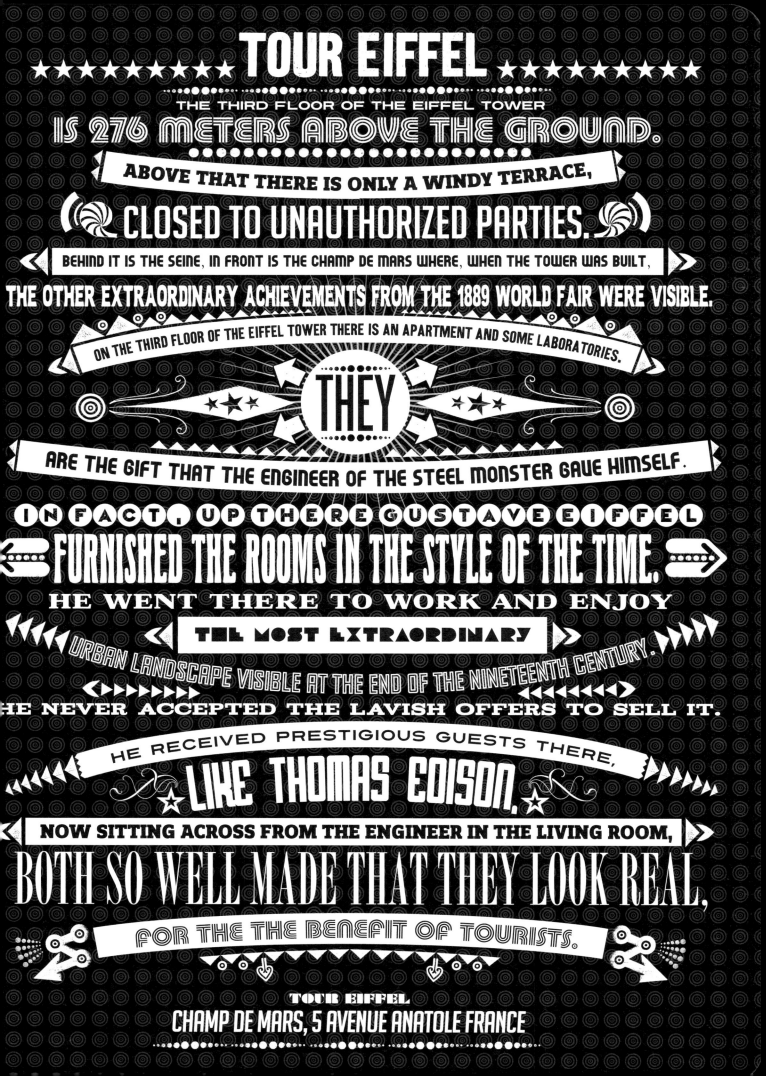

TOUR EIFFEL

★★★★★★★★★★★★★★★★★★★★★★★★

THE THIRD FLOOR OF THE EIFFEL TOWER

IS 276 METERS ABOVE THE GROUND.

ABOVE THAT THERE IS ONLY A WINDY TERRACE,

CLOSED TO UNAUTHORIZED PARTIES.

BEHIND IT IS THE SEINE, IN FRONT IS THE CHAMP DE MARS WHERE, WHEN THE TOWER WAS BUILT,

THE OTHER EXTRAORDINARY ACHIEVEMENTS FROM THE 1889 WORLD FAIR WERE VISIBLE.

ON THE THIRD FLOOR OF THE EIFFEL TOWER THERE IS AN APARTMENT AND SOME LABORATORIES.

THEY

ARE THE GIFT THAT THE ENGINEER OF THE STEEL MONSTER GAVE HIMSELF.

IN FACT, UP THERE GUSTAVE EIFFEL

FURNISHED THE ROOMS IN THE STYLE OF THE TIME.

HE WENT THERE TO WORK AND ENJOY

THE MOST EXTRAORDINARY

URBAN LANDSCAPE VISIBLE AT THE END OF THE NINETEENTH CENTURY.

HE NEVER ACCEPTED THE LAVISH OFFERS TO SELL IT.

HE RECEIVED PRESTIGIOUS GUESTS THERE,

LIKE THOMAS EDISON.

NOW SITTING ACROSS FROM THE ENGINEER IN THE LIVING ROOM,

BOTH SO WELL MADE THAT THEY LOOK REAL,

FOR THE THE BENEFIT OF TOURISTS.

TOUR EIFFEL

CHAMP DE MARS, 5 AVENUE ANATOLE FRANCE

Rue Saint-Dominique

Avenue de la Bourdonnais

Rue Fabert

Av de Suffren

Place Joffre

Av de Lowendal

Bl de Montparnasse

Boulevard Pasteur

Rue de Vaugirard

RESTAURANT LE PROCOPE ▶▶▶

13 RUE DE L'ANCIENNE COMÉDIE

FOUNDED IN 1689, THIS CAFE HAS SEEN MORE THAN THREE CENTURIES OF PARISIAN HISTORY. FRANCESCO PROCOPIO DEI COLTELLI CAME FROM SICILY AND BECAME A FRENCH CITIZEN, CHANGING HIS NAME TO FRANÇOIS PROCOPE COUTEAU. HE PURCHASED A BUILDING THAT HOUSED A PUBLIC BATHS, TURNING IT INTO A TAVERN. IN THE MEANTIME, COFFEE HAD COME TO PARIS A FEW YEARS EARLIER, THANKS TO THE TURKISH AMBASSADOR AND PROCOPE LINKED THE TAVERN TO A COFFEE HOUSE, FORMING THE SECOND CAFÈ GLACIER OF PARIS (THE FIRST HAD FAILED ALMOST IMMEDIATELY). PROCOPE WELCOMED VOLTAIRE AND THE ENTIRE ENCYCLOPAEDIA, ROUSSEAU, GENERALS, PHILOSOPHERS AND ACTORS. PROCOPE SAW THE REVOLUTION, THE GUILLOTINE, ROBESPIERRE, DANTON, NAPOLEON, THE NEW BOULEVARDS BY HAUSMANN AND MUCH MORE FROM HIS DOORS. THE WALLS WERE DECORATED WITH RED BROCADE, MIRRORS AND PAINTINGS, AND THERE WERE CRYSTAL LAMPS AND CUPS, MARBLES, TAPESTRIES, A GRAND STAIRCASE TO THE FIRST FLOOR, LARGE WINDOWS. JUST AS THEY ARE TODAY.

CAFE PROCOPE TENU PAR ZOPPI

MARIA DE MEDICI, QUEEN OF FRANCE DESPITE HER MANY ENEMIES, WAS THE PRINCIPLE CHARACTER IN THE AFFAIR OF THE JARDIN DU LUXEMBOURG: SHE WANTED A GARDEN FOR HER NEW RESIDENCE, THE PALAIS DU LUXEMBOURG. NOW TEN TIMES LARGER, THE LUXEMBOURG GARDENS ARE A MAGNIFICENT URBAN PARK ON THE RIVE GAUCHE OF THE RIVER SEINE. THE PALACE, WHICH FOR TWO YEARS SAW MARIA POSING FOR RUBENS, IS NOW HOME TO THE FRENCH SENATE. THE GARDENS HOST THOUSANDS OF ELMS, AVENUES, FLOWERBEDS AND BENCHES. THE MONUMENTAL FONTAINE MÉDICIS, WITH POLYPHEMUS SURPRISING ACIS AND GALATEA, AND A SMALL COPY OF THE STATUE OF LIBERTY STAND HERE, AND THERE ARE MANY OTHER STATUES, MUSEUMS, SCRAPS OF HISTORY AND ANECDOTES. ★★★

JARDIN DU LUXEMBOURG
2 RUE AUGUSTE COMTE

Rue Saint-Dominique

Bd Raspail

Sèvres

Rue du Cherche-Midi

Bd Saint-Germain

Rue d'Assas

Rue Saint-Michel

Rue Auguste Comte

PARIS

TALES OF A GRANDFATHER

THE SWAN PEN

PARIS

PARIS

◄◄◄◄◄◄◄◄ SAN FR

IN THE MEANTIME, THE BROTHELS WERE ALWAYS PACKED. THE CITY GREW, WITH MARKET STREET, CABLE CARS, CHINATOWN AND THE TRIADS. THEN THE GROUND TREMBLED. IT WAS APRIL 1906, JUST AFTER FIVE IN THE MORNING AND THE SKY WAS STILL DARK. THROUGHOUT THE DAY, ANYTHING THAT HAD REMAINED STANDING BURNED DOWN.

ANCISCO ▶▶▶▶▶▶

San Francisco Bay

Golden Gate Bridge

Golden Gate

Marina Blvd

Richardson Ave

Doyle Dr

Divisadero St

Lincoln Blvd

Veterans Blvd

Presidio Blvd

California St

Geary Blvd

Masonic Ave

Park Presidio Blvd

Geary Blvd

Fell St

Fulton St

Oak St

Masonic Ave

Stanyan St

Frederick St

Clayton St

19th Ave

GOLDEN GATE PARK
501 STANYAN STREET

SAN FRANCISCO CABLE CAR SYSTEM

San Francisco Bay

Bay St

The Embarcadero

Columbus Ave

Van Ness Ave

Fillmore St

California St

Geary Blvd

Fillmore St

The Embarcadero

Dwight D. Eisenhower Hwy

MECHANICS' INSTITUTE LIBRARY AND CHESS ROOM. 57 POST STREET

Market St

US-101

16th St

MISSION DOLORES CEMETERY 3321 16TH STREET

SAN FRANCISCO CABLE CAR SYSTEM

IT MAY LOOK LIKE A CHILDS TOY; A GREAT ENGINE ROOM WITH A STEAM ENGINE
THAT TURNS AN UNDERGROUND CABLE AND WAGONS THAT HOOK ONTO IT
AND ARE RELEASED WHEN THEY WANT TO STOP, BUT THE CABLE CARS CARRIED
SIXTY PASSENGERS TO THE TOP OF HILLS WHERE THE HORSES COULD NOT PULL
CARRIAGES OR WAGONS. BETWEEN 1873 AND 1890, MORE THAN TWENTY LINES
WERE BUILT. THEY BECAME OBSOLETE WITH THE ADVENT OF ELECTRIC MOTORS
AND INTERNAL COMBUSTION ENGINES, BUT TODAY THERE ARE THREE LINES,
COMPLETELY RENOVATED AND PERFECTLY WORKING.

MISSION DOLORES CEMETERY

MISSION DOLORES IS THE POPULAR NAME OF THE MISIÓN SAN FRANCISCO
DE ASÍS, ONE OF THE MOST NORTHERLY OF THE TWENTY-ONE MISSIONS BUILT
BY THE SPANISH FRANCISCANS IN EIGHTEENTH-CENTURY CALIFORNIA.
IN THE NEARBY CEMETERY MANY PEOPLE ARE BURIED, INCLUDING THE NUMEROUS
INDIGENOUS AMERICANS WHO ACTUALLY BUILT THE MISSION. UNDER THE SAME
TOMBSTONE LIE CHARLES CORA, AN ITALIAN EMIGRANT AND ARABELLA
"BELLE" RYAN, BOTH FROM BALTIMORE. HE WAS A GAMBLER,
SHE A PROSTITUTE; THEY CAME TOGETHER IN THE SEARCH FOR GOLD.
MISSION DOLORES CEMETERY - 3321 16TH STREET

GOLDEN GATE PARK

THE PARK WAS OPENED TO THE PUBLIC IN THE MID EIGHTEEN-SEVENTIES
AND STANDS ACROSS THE BAY NORTH OF THE CITY. A FEW YEARS LATER,
ON A SMALL HILL, THE CONSERVATORY OF FLOWERS WAS CREATED:
A GLASSHOUSE WITH A VICTORIAN-STYLE WOODEN STRUCTURE PAINTED
WHITE, AND A BOTANICAL GARDEN. AT THE TIME, THIS WAS PROBABLY THE
LARGEST GLASSHOUSE IN THE WORLD WITH ALMOST 17,000 PANES OF GLASS
AND A CENTRAL CUPOLA 18 METRES HIGH. THE OTHER ATTRACTIONS IN THE
PARK WERE (AND STILL ARE) THE JAPANESE GARDEN AND THE BISON PADDOCK,
BOTH OF WHICH DATE FROM THE EIGHTEEN-NINETIES.
GOLDEN GATE PARK - 501 STANYAN STREET

MECHANICS' INSTITUTE LIBRARY AND CHESS ROOM

ALTHOUGH IT IS COMPLETELY SURROUNDED BY SKYSCRAPERS, THE BUILDING OF
THE MECHANICS' INSTITUTE LIBRARY AND CHESS ROOM (1854) STILL
PRESERVES ITS MAGNIFICENCE. THERE WERE SOME BOOKS, A ROOM IN WHICH
TO PLAY CHESS, AND THE PLANS FOR A TECHNICAL SCHOOL IN A CITY WHERE
THERE WAS NOT EVEN A COLLEGE. IN THE TWILIGHT OF THE GOLD RUSH, SAN
FRANCISCO BECAME FULL OF DESTITUTE FAMILIES AND YOUNG PEOPLE WITHOUT
A FUTURE. THE MECHANICS' INSTITUTE, WITH ITS LESSONS AND ITS LIBRARY,
HELPED MANY OF THEM TO STUDY AND TO GROW.
MECHANICS' INSTITUTE LIBRARY AND CHESS ROOM - 57 POST STREET

119

SAINT PETERSBURG
MAY 1703, ON THE ORDERS OF THE TSAR PETER
THE GREAT, CONSTRUCTION WORK BEGAN ON A
FORTRESS ON THE ESTUARY OF THE RIVER NEVA AND
THE CITY OF SAINT PETERSBURG WAS BORN: DESIGNED AND
BUILT BY ARCHITECTS FROM CANTON TICINO AND FROM ITALY.
THROUGHOUT THE NINETEENTH CENTURY, IT WAS ONE OF THE MOST
IMPORTANT EUROPEAN CITIES. FRENCH WAS THE LANGUAGE SPOKEN
HERE, THE MUSIC OF RUSSIAN ROMANTICISM WAS WRITTEN HERE AND
THERE WERE RUMOURS OF WOULD-BE-REVOLUTIONARIES AND SECRET
SOCIETIES. THE AUTHOR PUSHKIN DIED IN A MEMORABLE RURAL DUEL. AS ANDREY
BELY WROTE, THE STREETS OF SAINT PETERSBURG HAVE AN UNDOUBTED QUALITY:
"THEY TRANSFORM PASSERS-BY INTO SHADOWS." SAINT PETERSBURG STANDS AT THE
POINT WHERE EUROPEAN CULTURE MEETS THE GELID WINDS FROM THE NORTH AND THE FIRST
TRACES OF THE SIBERIAN TAIGA. THE GREAT VACLAV NIJINSKY WAS NOT YET TWENTY WHEN HE
BROUGHT THE CHOREOGRAPHIES OF MARIUS PETIPA TO THE STAGE: IT WAS 1909 AND THE
PROTAGONISTS WERE CHANGING, IT WAS CLEAR THAT THE NINETEENTH CENTURY WAS CLOSING
ITS DOORS AND THE TWENTIETH CENTURY WAS TRULY STARTING. A BLANK SHOT FROM THE
CRUISER AURORA SIGNALLED THE START OF THE ASSAULT ON THE WINTER PALACE AND
OF THE GREATEST REVOLUTION OF THE TWENTIETH CENTURY.

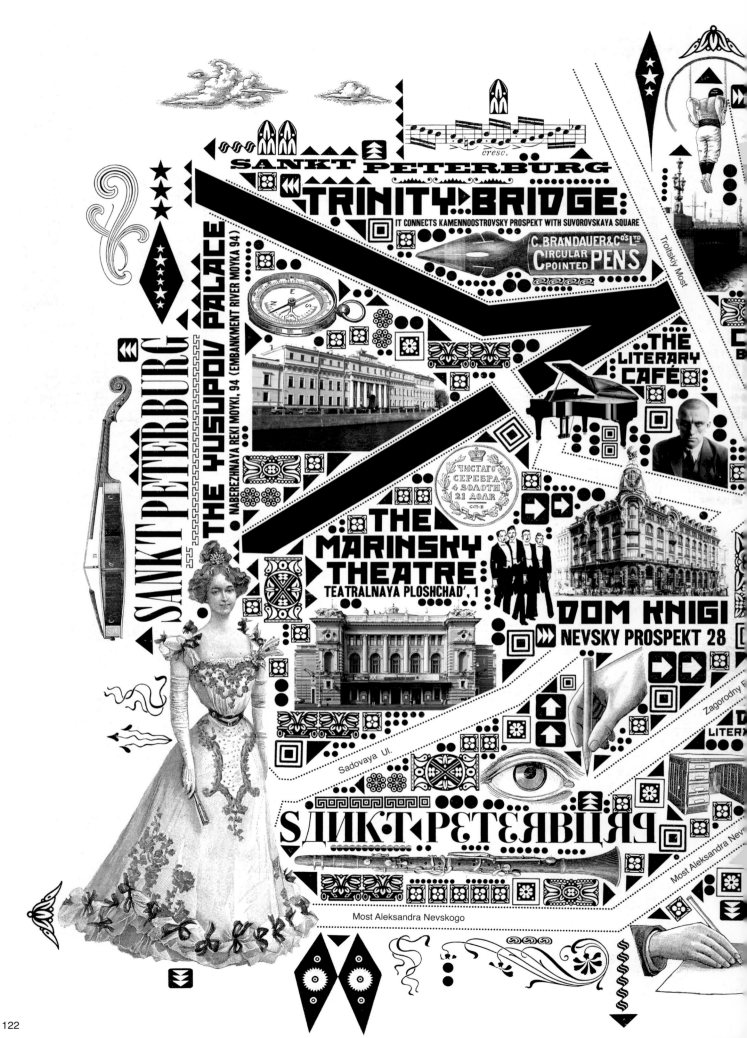

SANKT PETERBURG

TRINITY···BRIDGE:
IT CONNECTS KAMENNOOSTROVSKY PROSPEKT WITH SUVOROVSKAYA SQUARE

C. BRANDAUER & C°S LTD
CIRCULAR
POINTED PENS

Troitsky Most

THE
LITERARY
CAFÉ

SANKT PETERBURG

THE YUSUPOV PALACE

NABEREZHNAYA REKI MOYKI, 94 (EMBANKMENT RIVER MOYKA 94)

ЧИСТАГО
СЕРЕБРА
4 ЗОЛОТН
21 ДОЛР
С·П·Б

THE
MARINSKY
THEATRE
TEATRALNAYA PLOSHCHAD', 1

DOM KNIGI
NEVSKY PROSPEKT 28

Zagorodny P.

LITER

Sadovaya Ul.

SДИКТ·PETEЯВПЯЯ

Most Aleksandra Nev

Most Aleksandra Nevskogo

RET
CHAYA
AKA
JA ULITSA 5

SAGE
PROSPEKT 48

Liteyniy Ul.

NEVSKY PROSPEKT
NEVSKY PROSPEKT, FROM THE NEVA TO THE NEVA

Nevsky Ul.

SANKT PETERBURG

SANKT PETERBURG

JYEVSKY
RIAL MUSEUM
NY PEREULOK, 5/2

Ligovsky Ul.

Nevsky Ul.

Most Aleksandra Nevskogo

SДИКТ
PETEЯBЦЯЯ

Most Aleksandra Nevskogo

Ligovsky Ul.

TIKHVIN CEMETERY
PLACE ALEKSANDRA NEVSKOGO, IN THE PARK OF THE ALEXANDER NEVSKY MONASTERY

SANKT PETERBURG

THE YUSUPOV PALACE

THE MONUMENTAL PALACE OF THE YUSUPOV FAMILY
IS IN ITS ARCHITECTURE (INCLUDING THE FURNISHINGS)
ONE OF THE RICHEST AND BEST-PRESERVED ARISTOCRATIC
RESIDENCES FROM THE TSARIST PERIOD.
THE ORIGINAL CONSTRUCTION DATES FROM 1770.
THE VICISSITUDES OF THE PALACE EVEN INCLUDE A DETECTIVE STORY.
ON THE NIGHT OF DECEMBER 16TH 1916, IN ONE OF THE SALONS,
GRIGORY RASPUTIN, PERSONAL ADVISOR TO THE
TSAR AND THE TSARINA WAS KILLED BY THE PRINCE
FELIX YUSUPOV, LEADER OF A PLOT.
THE CORPSE WAS THROWN UNDER THE ICE ON THE NEVA
AND FOUND ONLY A FEW DAYS LATER. NO CERTAIN DETAILS
EMERGED FROM THE INQUIRIES: THE DEATH
OF RASPUTIN REMAINED A MYSTERY,
LIKE HIS PARANORMAL POWERS.
IN TWO ROOMS OF THE PALACE, THERE ARE LIFE-SIZE
WAX FIGURES TO RECALL THE EVENT.

NABERZHNAYA REKI MOYKI , 94

Trinity Bridge

IN A CITY BORN AND GROWN ON THE DELTA OF A RIVER, THE BRIDGES ARE NECESSARILY PROTAGONISTS, ALTHOUGH SOME ARE MORE IMPORTANT THAN OTHERS. AT SAINT PETERSBURG, AMONG THE LATTER IS THE TROITSKY MOST, OR TRINITY BRIDGE OVER THE NEVA, WHICH LINKS THE HISTORICAL CITY CENTRE AND THE ISLAND OF PETROGRADSKAYA. THERE HAS ALWAYS BEEN A BRIDGE HERE SINCE THE EARLY NINETEENTH CENTURY, BUT THE ONE WE CAN SEE TODAY WAS REBUILT AFTER THE SECOND WORLD WAR. IN THE NINETEEN-SIXTIES, IT BECAME A BASCULE BRIDGE: ONE OF ITS SPANS WAS REDESIGNED TO LIFT AND ALLOW LARGER BOATS TO PASS THROUGH. EVERY NIGHT, A SHOW OF LIGHT AND MOVEMENT IS GUARANTEED, ALSO DURING THE SUMMER ON THE WHITE NIGHTS, WHEN THE SKY NEVER DARKENS, SOME REMAIN IN THE BED OF THEIR LOVER, WITH THE EXCUSE THAT THEY CANNOT GO HOME, BECAUSE THE BRIDGE IS RAISED.

IT CONNECTS KAMENNOOSTROVSKY PROSPEKT WITH SUVOROVSKAYA SQUARE.

Tikhvin Cemetery

IN THE STEPPES OF CENTRAL ASIA IS A MUSICAL TABLEAU OR SYMPHONIC POEM, AND THE MUSICAL SCORE IS INSCRIBED ON THE FUNERARY MONUMENT OF ITS COMPOSER, ALEXANDER BORODIN. HE IS BEST KNOWN AS A COMPOSER AND MUSICIAN, BUT BORODIN WAS ABOVE ALL A CHEMIST, AN IMPORTANT MEMBER OF THE RUSSIAN MEDICAL-SURGICAL ACADEMY, AN EXCELLENT SCIENTIST, RESEARCHER AND PROFESSOR. HIS TOMB STANDS UNDER THE GREAT TREES OF THE TIKHVIN CEMETERY, ALONGSIDE THOSE OF GLINKA, MUSSORGSKY, RIMSKY-KORSAKOV, ANTON RUBINSTEIN, TCHAIKOVSKY, TO MENTION ONLY THE GREAT MUSICIANS, BUT ALSO DOSTOYEVSKY, EULER, STRAVINSKY'S FATHER, WHO WAS ALSO A MUSICIAN, MARIUS PETIPA, CARLO ROSSI, NATURALISED KARL IVANOVICH ROSSI, THE ARCHITECT OF HALF OF THE OLDER CITY OF SAINT PETERSBURG.

PLACE ALEKSANDRA NEVSKOGO, IN THE PARK OF THE ALEXANDER NEVSKY MONASTERY.

THE MARINSKY THEATRE

TEATRALNAJA PLOAD 1

OPENED IN 1860 AND EXTENDED IN 1885,
THE MARINSKY THEATRE
IS AN IMPORTANT PART
OF THE
HISTORY OF EUROPEAN MUSIC
FROM GLINKA TO MUSSORGSKY'S BORIS GODUNOV,
FROM SWAN LAKE TO THE NUTCRACKER
AND ALL
TCHAIKOVSKY'S
OTHER WORKS, UP TO RIMSKY-KORSAKOV,
THE GREAT RUSSIAN MUSIC
MADE ITS DEBUT HERE.
EVEN GIUSEPPE VERDI BROUGHT HIS
LA FORZA DEL DESTINO
HERE FOR ITS WORLD PREMIERE
ФИ 1862.

THE LITERARY CAFÉ
19 NEVSKY PROSPEKT

ALTHOUGH NOWADAYS IT IS THREATENED BY
THE HAMBURGERS OF AN ADJACENT BURGER KING,
THIS IS MERELY A GEOGRAPHICAL, DISRESPECTFUL,
AND CAPITALIST FACT, AND DOES NOT DISTURB THE
MEANING OF THE LITERATURNOE KAFE, ON THE CORNER OF NEVSKY
PROSPEKT, NEAR THE RIVER MOYKA, WHICH ENCIRCLES THE CENTRE
OF SAINT PETERSBURG, TRANSFORMING IT INTO AN ISLAND. SINCE
THE EIGHTEENTH CENTURY, THE BUILDING HAS BEEN A TAILORS SHOP,
A PATISSERIE, AND A CHINESE CAFÉ, PASSING THROUGH MANY HANDS INTO THOSE
OF THE KOTOMIN FAMILY, WHO BUILT THE COLUMNED PORTICO TO RIVAL THE FACING
BUILDING. DARK WALLS, CRYSTAL CHANDELIERS, PAINTINGS, BOOKCASES, UNEXPECTED
GREEN TABLE LAMPS, TABLECLOTHS, AND ALSO CURTAINS, WALL LIGHTS, AND PADDED
SEATING. ALL IN THE STYLE OF THE ERA OF PUSHKIN, DOSTOYEVSKY AND OTHERS.

IN 1910, THE SINGER MANUFACTURING COMPANY, WHICH ALREADY SOLD SEWING
MACHINES IN THE ENTIRE WORLD, BUILT THEIR RUSSIAN BRANCH IN SAINT PETERSBURG,
ON THE SITE OF AN EIGHTEENTH-CENTURY RESIDENTIAL BUILDING (WHERE THE
PHOTOGRAPHER SERGEI LEVITSKY DEVELOPED HIS DAGUERREOTYPES AND SOLD
EARLY PHOTOGRAPHIC EQUIPMENT). IT IS A SPLENDID EXAMPLE OF ART
NOUVEAU ARCHITECTURE. WHEN THE COMPANY LEFT, A YEAR AFTER THE
REVOLUTION, ALL THE RUSSIAN TAILORS WEPT. EVENTUALLY, THE
SINGER COMPANY BUILDING BECAME DOM KNIGI, THE HOUSE OF
THE BOOK. FIVE FLOORS OF PRINTED MATERIAL, DRAFTS,
AND CULTURE AT THE JUNCTION BETWEEN THE NEVSKY
PROSPEKT AND THE GRIBOEDOVA CANAL, FACING
THE KAZAN CATHEDRAL.

DOM KNIGI
NEVSKY PROSPEKT 28

BRODYACHAYA SOBAKA
ITALYANSKAYA ULITSA 5

"YOU, DWELLING FROM ORGY TO ORGY / HAVING BATHROOMS AND COSY WATER CLOSETS." MAYAKOVSKY IN HIS YELLOW SASH, STANDING ON A GREAT TABLE AT THE BRODYACHAYA SOBAKA, IN THE HALF-LIGHT OF THE CANDLES AND THE FIRST ELECTRIC LIGHTS, SCOURGED THE BOURGEOISIE AND THE ARISTOCRATS. PERHAPS IT IS ONLY A LEGEND, BUT IT WOULD NOT BE SURPRISING TO LEARN THAT THE BRODYACHAYA SOBAKA HAD ENJOYED A BRIEF, THRILLING SEASON BETWEEN THE NEW YEAR OF 1912 AND 1951, WHEN THE WORLD WAS TRANSFORMED INTO ONE IMMENSE TRENCH. IN THAT BASEMENT, ARTISTS AND REVOLUTIONARIES MET BY NIGHT, AND THEY ENCOUNTERED ANNA AKHMATOVA, WRAPPED IN BLACK SILK: "WE ARE ALL CAROUSERS AND LOOSE WOMEN HERE." TODAY THE SHADOWY BASEMENT IS STILL THERE, WITH POETS DECLAIMING THEIR VERSES.

THE NAME IS FRENCH, LIKE THE ARCHITECTURAL STYLE: A LONG COVERED GALLERY ON THREE STOREYS, LINED ON BOTH SIDES BY HUNDREDS OF LUXURY SHOPS AND BOUTIQUES. A EUROPEAN-STYLE SHOPPING ARCADE IN SAINT PETERSBURG, IN THE MID-NINETEENTH CENTURY. IT WAS 1864 WHEN IVAN MATVEICH AND HIS WIFE WENT TO THE PASSAGE, BECAUSE THEY HAD HEARD THAT A LIVE CROCODILE HAD ARRIVED, AND IT WAS EVEN POSSIBLE TO TOUCH IT. IT WAS THUS THAT ACCORDING TO DOSTOYEVSKY-IVAN MATVEICH WAS SWALLOWED ALIVE BY THE CROCODILE, UNDER THE GAZE OF WHITE MALAYAN PARROTS AND A TROOP OF MONKEYS. IN FACT, THE PRESENT CONSTRUCTION ACTUALLY DATES FROM THE NINETEEN-TWENTIES AND HAS NEVER SEEN A LIVE CROCODILE.

PASSAGE
NEVSKY PROSPEKT 48

DOSTOYEVSKY HOME AND MUSEUM

HUMILIATED AND INSULTED, CRIME AND PUNISHMENT, THE IDIOT, DEMONS, THE BROTHERS KARAMAZOV. THE GREATNESS OF FYODOR MIKHAILOVICH DOSTOYEVSKY IS EQUALLED ONLY BY THE COMPLEXITY AND DRAMATIC QUALITY OF HIS EARTHLY LIFE. IN THE MUSEUM DEDICATED TO HIM, WHICH IN 1971 OPENED IN THE SAINT PETERSBURG APARTMENT WHERE HE

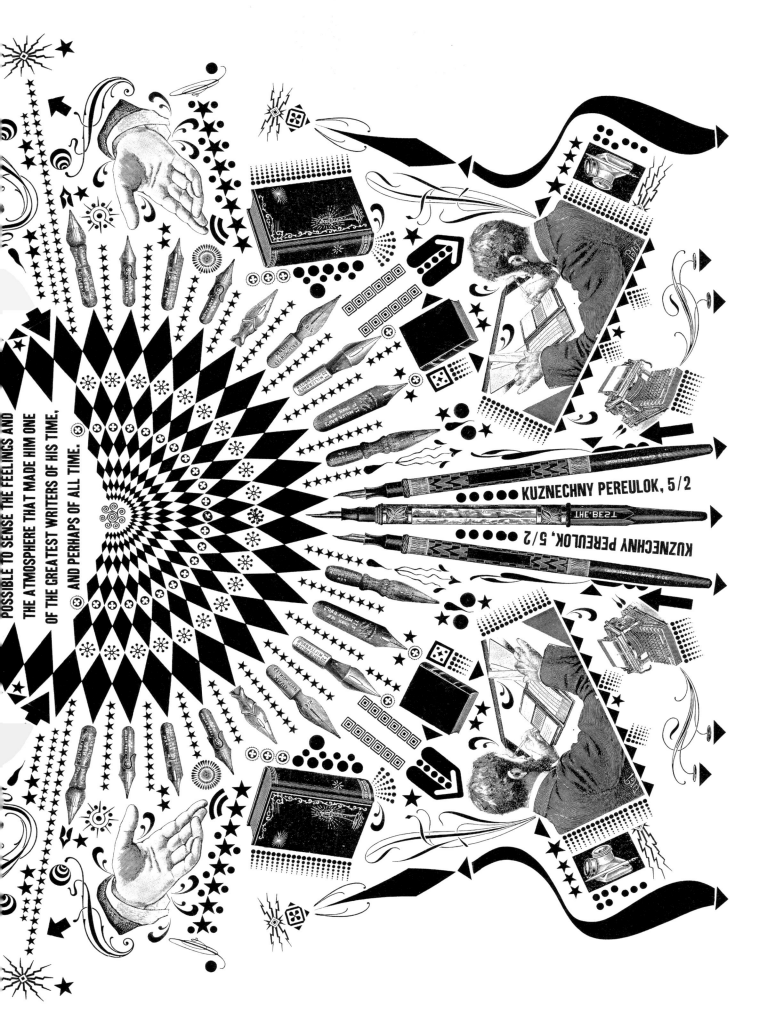

POSSIBLE TO SENSE THE FEELINGS AND
THE ATMOSPHERE THAT MADE HIM ONE
OF THE GREATEST WRITERS OF HIS TIME,
AND PERHAPS OF ALL TIME.

KUZNECHNY PEREULOK, 5/2

SHANGHAI

ONE OF THE MOST IMPORTANT PORTS IN CHINA FOR ABOUT A THOUSAND YEARS, SHANGHAI PLAYED A LEADING ROLE IN THE HISTORY OF THE COLONIAL PERIOD. THE BRITISH GUNBOATS RANGED THE COASTS

BRITISH PRESENCE IN THE FAR EAST AND THE REVOLTS AGAINST BRITISH TROOPS. AT THAT TIME, THE PORT BRISTLED WITH BROTHELS AND OPIUM DENS ON THE SAMPANS.

OF THE CHINA SEA OBSERVING A DECADENT EMPIRE AND AN IMMENSE COUNTRY IN DISARRAY. IN THE MID-NINETEENTH CENTURY SHANGHAI WAS STILL A LEADER IN THE DIRTY OPIUM TRADE, DURING THE

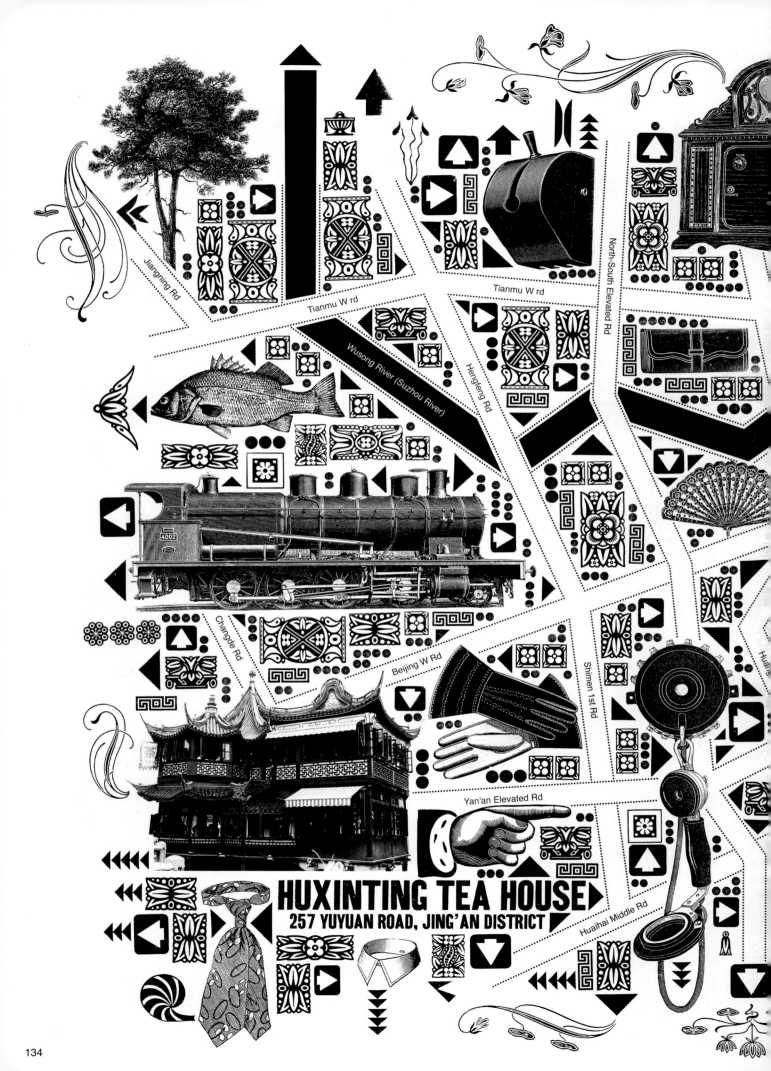

HUXINTING TEA HOUSE
257 YUYUAN ROAD, JING'AN DISTRICT

Jiangning Rd
Tianmu W rd
Tianmu W rd
North-South Elevated Rd
Hengfeng Rd
Wusong River (Suzhou River)
Changde Rd
Beijing W Rd
Shimen 1st Rd
Yan'an Elevated Rd
Huaihai Middle Rd

ASTOR HOUSE HOTEL
15 HUANGPU ROAD, HUANGPU DISTRICT

Haining Rd

Henan N Rd

Wusong River (Suzhou River)

Huangpu River

Beijing E Rd

Henan Middle Rd

Zhongshan East 1st Rd

ng W Rd

Xizang Middle Rd

Fuzhou Rd

Yan'an Elevated Tunnel

Yan'an Elevated Rd

nmin Ave

Yan'an Elevated Rd

Xizang S Rd

Renmin Rd

Henan S Rd

S Rd

YUYUAN GARDEN
218 ANREN STREET, HUANGPU DISTRICT

THE MANDARINS GARDEN HAS A HISTORY OF FOUR CENTURIES, AND A TROUBLED LIFE, IN CLEAR CONTRAST WITH THE ATMOSPHERE REQUIRED OF A GREEN OASIS IN THE MIDST OF THE CITY. MERCHANTS, CONQUERING ARMIES AND REBELS HAVE ALL TRAMPED THROUGH IT, BUT IN THE LAST CENTURY

IT FINALLY TOOK ON THE APPEARANCE THAT IT HAS NOW. FLOWERBEDS, PONDS, AND ABOVE ALL POETICALLY-NAMED PAVILIONS: THE PAVILION OF THE TEN THOUSAND FLOWERS, THE STUDY OF THE NINE LIONS, THE HALL OF JADE MAGNIFI-CENCE, THE PAVILION OF THE THREE EARS OF GRAIN, THE HALL HERALDING SPRING.

YUYUAN GARDEN
218 ANREN STREET, HUANGPU DISTRICT

THE BUILDINGS AND THE WALKWAYS THAT EMERGE FROM THE WATERS OF A SMALL ARTIFICIAL LAKE FORM THE STANDARD IMAGE OF A POSTCARD OF THE FAR EAST. THE SETTING IS TIMELESS, BUT THE TEA HOUSE PAVILION ONLY DATES FROM 1855,

AND WE OWE IT TO THE QING DYNASTYS EMPEROR XIANFENG.
IT STANDS IN THE OLD CITY: RED WOOD, LACQUER, DARK TABLES, LANTERNS, BOW WINDOWS. THERE IS ALSO A LONG ZIG-ZAG WALKWAY TO DISCOURAGE EVIL SPIRITS.

HUXINTING TEA HOUSE
257 YUYUAN ROAD, JING'AN DISTRICT

ASTOR HOUSE HOTEL

WHEN IT WAS OPENED IN 1846, IT WAS CALLED RICHARDS HOTEL AND RESTAURANT, AFTER ITS OWNER, AND IT WAS THE FIRST WESTERN-STYLE HOTEL IN THE FAR EAST. AT THE TIME, THE BRITISH NAVY HAD NO RIVALS. THE ASTOR HOUSE HOTEL WAS CALLED VICTORIAN, BUT ABOVE ALL, IT WAS LUXURIOUS. ITS EXTRAORDINARY BALLROOM WAS USED FOR PARTIES BY LONDON OFFICIALS AND FOR THE DEALINGS OF THE NEWBORN HONG KONG AND SHANGHAI BANKING CORPORATION.

15 HUANGPU ROAD, HUANGPU DISTRICT

NEISHIDI HOUSE

NEISHID

THE ORIGINAL BUILDING, PARTLY REBUILT AND TOTALLY REFURBISHED AT THE START OF CENTURY, IS SOME HUNDREDS OF YEARS OLD, BUT IT BECAME PART OF HISTORY IN THE EAR TWENTIETH CENTURY, WHEN IT SAW THE BIRTH OF THE WIFE OF SUN YAT-SEN, THE HIS

HOUSE

...CAL AND IDEOLOGICAL FATHER OF POST-IMPERIAL CHINA. IT LATER HOSTED OTHER ...EAT FIGURES OF THE REVOLUTION AND OF CHINESE CULTURE. FURNITURE, DOCUMENTS, ...OTOGRAPHS FROM A DISTANT WORLD, TODAY SILENT, BUT ONCE EXPLOSIVE.

VIENNA

WALTZES AND WONDERFUL MUSIC, FROM THE DEEP NOTES OF BEETHOVEN TO THE MERRY WIDOWS OF LEHÁR. IT WAS THE NINETEENTH CENTURY AND VIENNA SHARED WITH BERLIN THE TITLE OF CAPITAL OF MITTELEUROPE AND WITH PARIS THAT OF CAPITAL OF EUROPEAN MUSIC. THE MOST IMPERIAL FAMILY

OF EUROPE AND THE BRUSHES AND EASELS OF THE VIENNA SECESSION ART MOVEMENT WERE ALL ITS OWN. ITS BORDERS TOUCHED ON THE OTTOMAN EMPIRE AND LAPPED ON THE ENDLESS RUSSIAN STEPPES. ONLY THE FIRST WORLD WAR WOULD CHANGE ALL THIS, AS IT CHANGED ALMOST THE ENTIRE WORLD.

· VIENNA ·

VIENNA

SIGMUND FREUD MUSEUM
STEPHANSPLATZ 3
INNERE STADT

CHOCOLAT

Türkenstraße

Hörlgasse

Schottenring

ANKE
THE M
ANKERU

Garnisongasse

Währinger Straße

Alser Straße

Universitätsstraße

RINGSTRASSE

STYLISH TOIL
JUGENDSTIL-TOILETTE AM
GRABEN, NEAR KOHL
INNERE

WC

Landesgerichtsstraße

Universitätsring

Josefstädter Straße

CAFÉ

Auerspergstraße

Museumstraße

DEMEL AND
HOTEL SACHER
DEMEL K.U.K. HOFZUCKERBÄCKER WIEN
KOLHMARKT 14, INNERE STADT;
HOTEL SACHER WIEN
PHILHARMONIKERSTRASSE 4, INNERE STADT

Burggasse

Burgring

Opernring

Museumsplatz

Kärntner Ring

Getreidemarkt

Friedrichstraße

Karlsplatz

Karlsplatz

VIE
NNA

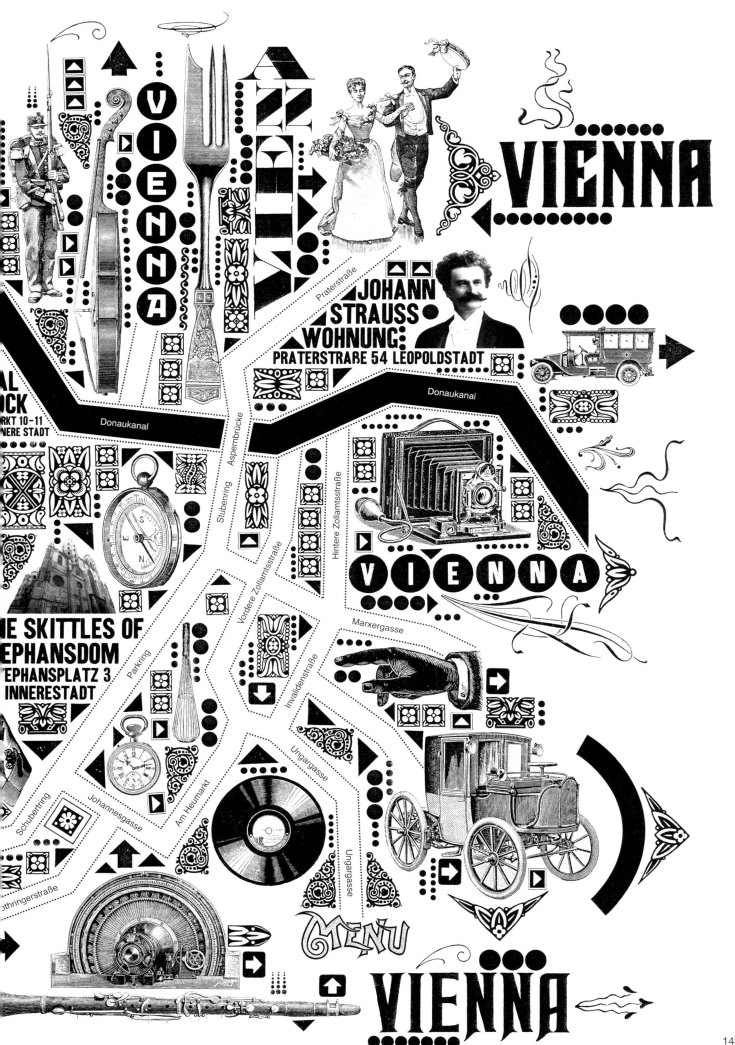

VIENNA

VIENNA

WIEN

VIENNA

JOHANN
STRAUSS
WOHNUNG
PRATERSTRAßE 54 LEOPOLDSTADT

Praterstraße

Donaukanal

Donaukanal

VIENNA

AL
OCK
RKT 10–11
ERE STADT

E SKITTLES OF
EPHANSDOM
EPHANSPLATZ 3
INNERESTADT

Stubenring

Aspernbrücke

Hintere Zollamtsstraße

Vordere Zollamtsstraße

Marxergasse

Invalidenstraße

Parkring

Ungargasse

Ungargasse

Am Heumarkt

Johannesgasse

Schubertring

othringerstraße

MENU

VIENNA

"... HOUSE A FINE MUSEUM."

↑ THE MUSICIAN, DEDICATED TO THE MUSICIAN,

DOCUMENTS AND MEMORABILIA DEDICATED TO THE MUSICIAN,

...RNISHINGS ON DISPLAY, BUT ALSO PAINTINGS,

"... THERE ARE MUSICAL INSTRUMENTS

R WORLD-FAMOUS WALTZ. ...

R HENRIETTE TREFFZ, HERE, IN 1867,

...ARTMENT FOR SEVEN YEARS WITH HIS FIRST WIFE,

...MEMBER OF THE TALENTED STRAUSS FAMILY

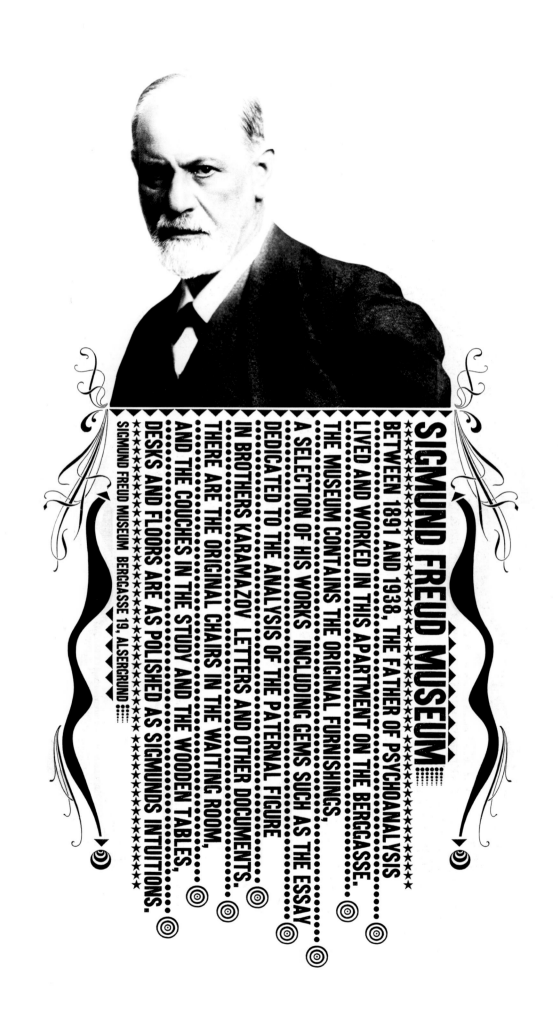

SIGMUND FREUD MUSEUM

BETWEEN 1891 AND 1938, THE FATHER OF PSYCHOANALYSIS
LIVED AND WORKED IN THIS APARTMENT ON THE BERGGASSE.
THE MUSEUM CONTAINS THE ORIGINAL FURNISHINGS,
A SELECTION OF HIS WORKS INCLUDING GEMS SUCH AS THE ESSAY
DEDICATED TO THE ANALYSIS OF THE PATERNAL FIGURE
IN BROTHERS KARAMAZOV LETTERS AND OTHER DOCUMENTS.
THERE ARE THE ORIGINAL CHAIRS IN THE WAITING ROOM,
AND THE COUCHES IN THE STUDY AND THE WOODEN TABLES,
DESKS AND FLOORS ARE AS POLISHED AS SIGMUNDS INTUITIONS.

SIGMUND FREUD MUSEUM, BERGGASSE 19, ALSERGRUND

146

DEMEL AND HOTEL SACHER

1832: ON THE OCCASION OF A RECEPTION HELD BY THE EMPEROR, FRANZ SACHER CREATED A CHOCOLATE CAKE WITH APRICOT JAM THAT WOULD BECOME THE SWEETEST SYMBOL OF VIENNA, TOGETHER WITH THE PRINCESS SISI, WHO LOVED IT.

1860 AB: AT THE FAMOUS PASTRY SHOP DEMEL HIS SON, EDUARD SACHER, PERFECTED THE RECIPE AS THE EDUARD SACHER-TORTE.

1876: EDUARD SACHER OPENED THE ELEGANT HOTEL SACHER IN THE CAPITAL AND THE PASTRY SHOP OF THE SAME NAME BEGAN TURNING OUT THOUSANDS OF ORIGINAL SACHER-TORTE.

DEMEL K.U.K. HOFZUCKERBÄCKER WIEN – KOHLMARKT 14, INNERE STADT ● HOTEL SACHER WIEN – PHILHARMONIKERSTRAE 4, INNERE STADT

RINGSTRAßE

RINGSTRAßE

FOLLOWING A DECREE BY FRANZ JOSEPH I, IN THE MID-NINETEENTH CENTURY THE ANCIENT CITY WALLS OF VIENNA WERE TRANSFORMED INTO A WIDE CIRCULAR BOULEVARD THAT EVERYONE WOULD SIMPLY CALL THE RING. THE HABSBURG IMPERIAL PALACE OVERLOOKS THE RINGSTRASSE, AS DO THEATRES, MUSEUMS, CAFES, THE OPERA HOUSE, PARKS, SQUARES AND THE UNIVERSITY. THERE ARE ALSO THE MAGNIFICENT PALACES OF THE OLD ARISTOCRACY AND THE NEW BOURGEOISIE. IT IS IMPOSSIBLE TO GET LOST IN VIENNA, BECAUSE SOONER OR LATER YOU WILL FIND YOURSELF ON RINGSTRASSE, BECAUSE THE RINGSTRASSE IS EVERYWHERE.

JUGENDSTIL-TOILETTE AM GRABEN
GRABEN, NEAR KOHLMARKT, INNERE STADT

IN 1880, BEETZ, INSPIRED BY OTHER EUROPEAN CITIES, LIKE LONDON, PRESENTED A PROPOSAL TO EQUIP THE CITY WITH PUBLIC TOILETS. IN 1883, AFTER RECEIVING AUTHORISATION, HE FOUNDED A COMPANY THAT IS STILL OPERATING, PERSONALLY SUPERVISING THE CONSTRUCTION OF THE TOILETS (THE FIRST WAS IMPORTED FROM BERLIN) AND THEIR FUNDING-HE PAID FOR WATER, ELECTRICITY AND GAS. LATER, IN 1905, THE ARCHITECT LOOS BUILT THE PUBLIC TOILETS AT GRABEN, IN JUGENDSTIL. THEY ARE STILL OPERATIVE.

ANKERUHR - THE MUSICAL CLOCK

HOHER MARKT 10-11, INNERE STADT

AT MIDDAY, TWELVE HISTORICAL FIGURES FROM MARCO AURELIUS, THE FIRST GOVERNOR OF THE ANCIENT VINDOBONA
TO JOSEPH HAYDN AND EVEN CHARLEMAGNE AND MARIE THERESE OF AUSTRIA PARADE BEFORE THE TOURISTS ON THE MAGNIFICENT
ART NOUVEAU DIAL OF THE ANKERUHR. THEY ARE ACCOMPANIED BY HAYDNS MELODY DIE HIMMEL ERZÄHLEN DIE EHRE GOTTES,
WHICH REPLACED THE HYMN TO THE EMPEROR WHEN THE AUSTRO-HUNGARIAN EMPIRE DECLINED.
THIS MECHANICAL CLOCK WAS BUILT BETWEEN 1911 AND 1917 BY THE VIENNESE PAINTER FRANZ VON MATSCH.

ZENTRALFRIEDHOF

SIMMERINGER HAUPTSTRAßE 230-244, SIMMERING

IT IS SAID IN VIENNA THAT THE ZENTRALFRIEDHOF "IS ALMOST AS WIDE AS THE CITY OF ZURICH, BUT IT IS TWICE AS MUCH FUN."
CERTAINLY THE CENTRAL CEMETERY (INAUGURATED IN 1874), WHICH EXTENDS FOR 2.5 SQUARE KILOMETRES AND HOUSES MORE THAN
THREE MILLION TOMBS, INCLUDING THOSE OF SALIERI, BEETHOVEN, BRAHMS, STRAUSS, SCHUBERT AND SCHÖNBERG, IS UNUSUAL,
SINCE IT HAS SEPARATE SECTIONS FOR CATHOLICS, PROTESTANTS, ORTHODOX CHRISTIANS, MUSLIMS AND TWO JEWISH CEMETERIES.

INDEX OF PEOPLE

ABDUL-AZIZ, 62
AKHMATOVA, ANNA, 129

BARNUM'S CIRCUS, 97
BEETHOVEN, LUDWIG VAN, 141, 149
BEETZ, WILHELM, 148
BELY, ANDREY, 121
BERNHARDT SARAH, 5, 47
BONAPARTE, NAPOLEON, 27, 113
BOOTH, EDWIN, 99
BORODIN, ALEXANDER, 126
BOTTICELLI, SANDRO, 74, 86
BRAHMS, JOHANNES, 149
BUONARROTI, MICHELANGELO, 74

CARUSO, ENRICO, 5, 88, 96
CATTANEO, CARLO, 82, 87
CAVOUR, CAMILLO BENSO, CONTE DI, 82
CÉZANNE, PAUL, 74
CHARLEMAGNE, 149
CHENG I, 57
CHEUNG CHAU, 56
CHEUNG PO TSAI, 56
CHEVALIER, MAURICE, 109
CHOPIN, FRYDERYK FRANCISZEK, 5
CHRISTIE, AGATHA, 5, 63
CHURCHILL, WINSTON, 40
CORA, CHARLES, 117

D'ANTHÈS, GEORGES, 5
DANTON, GEORGES JACQUES, 113
DICKENS, CHARLES, 68
DORABJEE NAOROJEE MITHAIWALA, 54
DOSTOYEVSKY, FYODOR MIKHAILOVICH, 16,
128, 129, 130-1
DOYLE, ARTHUR CONAN, 77
DRACULA, 74
DUPIN, AMANTINE-LUCILE-
AURORE DUPIN V. SAND, GEORGE
DVORAK, ANTONIN, 77

EDISON, THOMAS, 111
EIFFEL, GUSTAVE, 111
EUGENIE OF FRANCE, EMPRESS, 62
EULER, LEONARD, 126

FRANZ JOSEPH, 148
FREUD, SIGMUND, 146

GARCIA LORCA, FEDERICO, 47
GARIBALDI, GIUSEPPE, 82
GAUDÌ, ANTONI, 14-15
GEORGE IV, 72
GIGLI, BENIAMINO, 85
GLINKA, MICHAIL IVANOVICH, 126, 127
GRAVES & DUBOY, ARCHITECTS, 96

HAUSMANN, GEORGES EUGÉNE, BARON, 113
HAYDN, JOSEPH, 149
HOLMES, SHERLOCK, 68

JACK THE RIPPER, 68
JONES, EDWARD, 73

KALBO FAMILY, 27
KOTOMIN FAMILY, 128

LA BELLE OTERO, 109
LEHÁR, FRANZ, 141
LEVITSKY, SERGEI, 128
LIEBERMANN, MAX, 22
LINCOLN, ABRAHAM, 99
LOOS, ADOLF, 148
LOTI, PIERRE, 64

MACEO, ANTONIO, 47
MADAME CHING, 57
MAN CHUNG-LUEN, 57
MANET, EDOUARD, 109
MANTEGNA, ANDREA, 86
MANZONI, ALESSANDRO, 82, 87
MARCO AURELIUS, 149
MARIA DE MEDICI, 113
MARIE THERESE OF AUSTRIA, 149
MARX, KARL, 5, 74
MATVEICH, IVAN, 129
MAYAKOVSKY, VLADIMIR, 129
MISTINGUETT, 109
MONET, CLAUDE, 74
MUSSORGSKY, MODEST PETROVICH, 126, 127

NESBIT, EVELYN, 99

PAGANINI, NICCOLÒ, 85
PAOLO UCCELLO, 74
PETER THE GREAT, TSAR, 121
PETIPA, MARIUS, 121, 126
PIERO DELLA FRANCESCA, 74, 86
POLDI PEZZOLI, GIAN GIACOMO, 86
PRINCE ALBERT, 74
PRINCE FELIX YUSUPOV, 125
PRINCESS SISI, 147
PROCOPE COUTEAU, FRANÇOIS, 113
PROUST, MARCEL, 109
PUCCINI, GIACOMO, 84
PUSHKIN, ALEKSANDR SERGEEVICH, 4, 5, 121, 128

QUASIMODO, SALVATORE, 87
QUEEN VICTORIA, 69, 72, 73, 74

RAPHAEL, 74
RASPUTIN, GRIGORI, 125
REMBRANDT, 74
RHODES, CECIL, 40, 41
RIMSKY-KORSAKOV, NICOLAY ANDREEVICH,
126, 127
ROBESPIERRE, MAXIMILIEN DE, 113
ROSSI, CARLO, 126
ROSSINI, GIOACCHINO, 84
ROUSSEAU, JEAN-JACQUES, 113
RUBENS, PIETER PAUL, 113
RUBINSTEIN, ANTON, 126
RYAN, ARABELLA "BELLE", 117

SACHER, EDUARD, 147
SACHER, FRANZ, 147
SALIERI, ANTONIO, 149
SAND, GEORGE, 5
SCHEIDEMANN, PHILIP, 25
SCHÖNBERG, ARNOLD, 149
SCHUBERT, FRANZ PETER, 149
STENDHAL, 85
STODDART, JOSEPH MARSHALL, 77
STRAUSS, JOHANN, 144-5, 149
STRAVINSKY, IGOR, 96, 126
SUN YAT-SEN, 138

TAMAGNO, FRANCESCO, 89
TCHAIKOVSKY, PYOTR ILYICH, 126, 127
TONGZHI, EMPEROR, 57
TOSCANINI, ARTURO, 84, 96
TOULOUSE LAUTREC, HENRI, 109
TREFFZ, HENRIETTE, 144-5
TURNER, JOSEPH MALLORD WILLIAM, 74
TWAIN, MARK, 77

VAN GOGH, VINCENT, 74
VAN RIEBEECK, JAN, 41
VERDI, GIUSEPPE, 82, 88, 89, 127
VERMUYDEN, BARTHOLOMEUS, 41
VITTORIO EMANUELE II, 79
VOLTAIRE, 113
VON BISMARK, OTTO 24
VON MATSCH, FRANZ, 149

WATTS, GEORGE FREDERIC, 75
WHITE, STANFORD, 99
WILDE, OSCAR, 77
WILHELM I, 24
WILHELM II, 24
WILKES, JOHN, 99

XIANFENG, EMPEROR, 136

ZARATHUSTRA, 54

INDEX OF PLACES

ADDERLEY STREET FOUNTAIN, 41
AMERICAN MUSEUM OF NATURAL HISTORY, 98
ANKERUHR, 149
ANSONIA BUILDING, 96
ASTOR HOUSE HOTEL, 137

BEYAZIT TOWER, 65
BEYLERBENI PALACE, 62
BIERGARTEN PRATER, 27
BRANDENBURGER TOR, 26, 27
BRIGHTON BEACH, 99
BRITISH MUSEUM, 74
BRODJAAJA SOBAKA CABARET, 128
BROOKLYN BRIDGE, 97
BUCKINGHAM PALACE, 72-73
BUNDESTAG, 24-25

CAFÉ PROCOPE, 113
CAFÉ TORTONI, 34-35
CAFFÉ CAMPARINO, 83
CAFFÉ MIANI, 83
CAPE OF GOOD HOPE, 39
CAPE TOWN CLUB, 40
CASA MANZONI, 82
CASA ROSADA, 34
CASTELL DELS TRES DRAGONS, 16
CHARLES DICKENS MUSEUM, 75
CHEUNG PO TSAI CAVE, 56-57
CIMITERO MONUMENTALE, 87
CONEY ISLAND, 99
CONSERVATORY OF FLOWERS, 119
CRITERION THEATRE, 75

DEMEL AND HOTEL SACHER, 147
DOM KNIGI, 128
DOSTOYEVSKY HOME AND MUSEUM, 130-131

EL ATENEO GRAND SPENDID, 30
EL MALECÓN, 46
ENGINE 55, 101

FLATIRON BUILDING, 98
FOLIES BERGÈRE, 108-109
FONTAINE MÉDICIS, 113

GALLERIA VITTORIO EMANUELE, 83
GARDENS OF THE MINISTRY OF WAR, 65
GOLDEN GATE PARK, 119
GRAN TEATRO DE LA HABANA ALICIA ALONSO, 47
GRAND HOTEL ET DE MILAN, 88-89
GRIBOEDOVA CANAL, 128

HEERENGRACHT STREET, 41
HIGHGATE, 7
HONG KONG MARITIME MUSEUM, 55
HOTEL INGLATERRA, 47
HUMBOLDT-UNIVERSITÄT ZU BERLIN, 26
HUXINTING TEA HOUSE, 136

JARDIN DU LUXEMBOURG, 113
JOHANN STRAUSS WOHNUNG, 144-145
JUGENDSTIL-TOILETTE AM GRABEN, 148

KAZAN CATHEDRAL, 128

LANGHAM HOTEL, 77
LIEBERMANN VILLA, 22
LION'S HEAD MOUNTAIN, 39
LONDON PAVILION, 75
LONG STREET, 41

MAN MO TEMPLE, 56
MARINSKY THEATRE, 127
MECHANICS' INSTITUTE, 119
MERCAT DE GALVANY, 17
MISSION DOLORES CEMETERY, 117
MOUNT NELSON HOTEL, 40
MUSEO POLDI PEZZOLI, 86
MUSEUM FÜR KOMMUNIKATION, 26
MUSEUMSINSEL, 26

NATIONAL GALLERY, 74
NEISHIDI HOUSE, 138-139
NEVSKY PROSPEKT, 128, 129

OLD STAR FERRY PIER, 54-55

PALACIO DE AGUAS CORRIENTES, 31
PALAIS DU LUXEMBOURG, 113
PASSAGE, 129
PEARL RIVER, 50
PERA PALACE HOTEL, 63
PICCADILLY CIRCUS, 75
PIERRE LOTI CAFÉ, 64
PLAZA DE MAYO, 34
POSTMAN'S PARK, 75
PRINCESS LOUISE PUB, 74

REGENT STREET, 75
RINGSTRASSE, 148
RIVER MOYKA, 128
RIVER NEVA, 121, 126
RIVER SEINE, 111, 113
RIVER SPREE, 19
RIVER THAMES, 69

SAGRADA FAMILIA, 14-15
SAINT PANCRAS STATION, 76
SAINT PAUL'S CATHEDRAL, 75
SAN FRANCISCO CABLE CAR SYSTEM, 117
SCOTLAND YARD, 74
SIGMUND FREUD MUSEUM, 146
SINGER MANUFACTURING COMPANY, 128
STAATSBIBLIOTHEK ZU BERLIN, 26
STAATSOPER, 26
STATUE OF JAN VAN RIEBEECK, 41
SUEZ CANAL, 62

TABLE MOUNTAIN, 39
TAI FU TAI MANSION, 57
TEATRO ALLA SCALA, 82, 83, 84-85
TEATRO COLÓN, 31
THE CITY CLUB, 40
THE CIVIL SERVICE CLUB, 40
THE DUOMO, 82
THE LITERARY CAFÉ, 128
THE PLAYERS CLUB, 99
TIERGARTEN, 26
TIKHVIN CEMETERY, 126
TOUR EIFFEL, 16, 110-111
TRINITY BRIDGE, 126

UNIVERSITY OF ISTANBUL, 65
UNTER DEN LINDEN, 26

YUSUPOV PALACE, 125
YUYUAN GARDEN, 136

ZENTRALFRIEDHOF, 149